Hubert S Weiner
August 1976
Pointe Claire

LOGGING

LOGGING

British Columbia's Logging History

Ed Gould

ISBN 0-919654-44-4

Copyright © 1975   Ed Gould

DESIGNED BY NICHOLAS NEWBECK DESIGN

PRINTED IN CANADA

Canadian Shared Cataloguing in Publication Data
Gould, Ed
     Logging; British Columbia's logging history
     1. Lumbering - British Columbia - history
I. Title.
[SD538.3.C2G69]   634.9'82'09711
ISBN 0-919654-44-4

HANCOCK HOUSE PUBLISHERS LTD.
3215 Island View Road
Saanichton, British Columbia, Canada

Contents

TO MY MOTHER
from an appreciative son

The author would like to thank a number of people who assisted in the writing and research of this book. Without them it would not have been possible. Any errors of omission or commission are, however, mine.

Acknowledgments

Jean Sorenson, Assistant Editor of *B.C. Lumberman* magazine, gave me a number of useful articles and names of people to contact for information and photographs. Derek Reimer, Assistant Director of the Aural History Division of the Provincial Archives, allowed me unlimited access to his files on logging and related subjects. Jeanette Taylor of that department was also helpful.

Since the collecting of photographs was a very important part of the task, I am grateful to J. Robert Davison, Director of Visual Records at the Provincial Archives, to his Assistant, Barbara MacLennan, and to members of the production staff who always do such fine photographic reproduction.

Barbara Davies and Peter Robin at British Columbia Forest Service also helped supply photographs. Lynn Ogden and his staff at Vancouver City Archives and Director Ron D'Altroy and Assistant Jacquie Stevens at Vancouver Public Library were very helpful in locating photographs.

There are several outstanding individuals within the forest industry who were generous with their time and assistance: Sue Baptie, Archivist and Historian at British Columbia Forest Products; Jim Bogyo, Director of Public Relations at Rayonier Canada (B.C.) Limited; Dennis Bell and Nicky Gillies at MacMillan Bloedel; Jack Morris of External Information Services at Crown Zellerbach Canada Limited; Joe McKinnon and Donna M. du Bois at the Council of Forest Industries and H. H. Crompton at Seaspan International Ltd.

Thanks are also offered to Ken McEwan of the Duncan local of International Woodworkers of America and Tom Fawkes of the IWA head office in Vancouver. Owen Hennigar, Ray Bailey, Jack Vetleson and Gordon Flowerdew of Canadian Forest Products extended hospitality and useful information while I was visiting Woss Camp and Beaver Cove. Special thanks to Tonia Baney for giving me permission to quote from her material collected for an excellent visual history of logging in British Columbia. Also to Chester Richard Matheson for permission to quote from his unpublished thesis on log towing.

Helen T. Richards of Gibsons Brothers Industries Ltd. and Enid Lemon, librarian at B.C. Forest Service pointed out useful sources of information. Ray Wormald, Hugh Lyons and Doug Adderley at the Forest Service were also helpful, particularly Mr. Lyons who read parts of the manuscript and made suggestions. Frank Waters of the Council of Forest Industries gave unstintingly of his time and vast knowledge of logging.

Finally, a note of appreciation for the sterling efforts of Elizabeth Minifie for her skill and patience in editing the whole manuscript, and to my wife Jan who took time out from writing her own book to do some research for me.

No list of credits could be complete without mentioning the hundreds of loggers and millworkers, union leaders and company representatives who—without exception—gave freely of their time to tell this story. Pleasing them would be the highest form of compliment.

ED GOULD
Victoria, B.C.
September, 1975

7

Steam locie and trainload of logs.

8

1.
Tin Pants and Whistle Punks
Colorful terms and colorful men.

The British Columbian who works in the woods is not a *lumberjack.* He is a lumberjack only in novels by retired teachers, by writers who have never been out of Vancouver, by Americans and by eastern journalists. A man who works in the woods in B.C. is a *logger.* He may also answer to *ape* or *bush ape,* and if he quits and takes a job in a mill, *tame ape.*

His language is strong and strange. The strong part is usually saved for the bush or the beer parlor; the strange part he can't repress because it's as much a part of him as his *tin pants,* his unbending waterproofs. Some of his terms and phrases have been handed down over the years, others are fairly recent, and the word-building goes on.

The logging industry has a rich background to draw upon. Take bulls, for example: Bulls were used almost from the start and calling the drover or teamster a *bullpusher* seemed to put wordsmiths into a frenzy because after that they were full of bull: *Bull of the Woods* (woods boss or owner); *bullbucker* (foreman or supervisor of the cutting crew); *bullpen* (where unsorted logs are dumped); *bulldozer* (tracked machines used for clearing roads or yarding logs); *bullchokers* (used when extra strength is needed to move heavy logs or overcome a *hangup*—which has nothing to do with your neuroses) and *bullcook,* that handyman around the camp.

If you hear a logger talking about a *show,* chances are it's a *railroad show,* a *truck show* or maybe, a *skyline show.* There are no movies or dancing girls at these shows; the term refers to the piece of country being logged or the method being used.

If a logger is just starting out in his chosen career, he'll likely be put *setting chokers*, that is, placing a cable around logs ("choking" them) so they can be *yarded* into the *spar tree*, a trimmed and topped tree which has been rigged with blocks and cables so the donkey engine can "yard" the logs out of the bush. The *chokerman* works under the loving care and guidance of a *hooktender* who is also a *hooker*, but not of the happy variety, although he may occasionally smile, such as when the poor novice is sent off to get a *bucket of steam*, a *left-handed hammer*, to *oil a skyhook* or catch a *sackful of chokerholes*. All but the choker-holes are imaginary articles dreamed up by skylarking loggers. The chokerhole is a space the chokerman may have to dig in order to get his choker around a log.

Our hero is driven to work in a *crummy*, a bus that transports loggers to the job site. He hopes today he'll get the *candy side*, a *unit* that's a piece of cake compared with that *suicide show* he worked yesterday which was staged on a sidehill, all gullies, underbrush and *widow-makers*, trees with dead tops or trees that have fallen into other trees. He doesn't want to leave camp *feet first*: dead.

Actually, this is a pretty *skookum* camp. But he'd better *cut it* here or the *super* will tell him to *pick up his time*. Yesterday he really *gave her snoose, let 'er rip, highballed it*. Those other apes know he's got the *stuff*. It's not like that *haywire gyppo* where he *pulled the pin* last month. He *packed it in*, quit, because the independent operation was run on a shoestring. They had a *boom chain* for a *bull block strap*, for cry sake!

And the *push* on that *raft camp*, a floating operation built on logs, was always yelling: "On the ball or on the boat!" He got on the boat—when it eventually came—because he was *bushed* and *stakey*—too long in isolation and money burning a hole in his pocket. The food at that camp was rotten. The cook was a *gutburner*, a *bean burner*, a *meat burner* and a *canopener artist*. He cooked nothing but *cackleberries*, *hen fruit*, that is, eggs, and *Klondike spuds*, raw potatoes fried in the pan. No *sow bosom* at least. Salt pork is thankfully a thing of the past. And the *monkey blankets* were okay. You can't do much wrong to a flapjack, hotcake, pancake. They weren't your Aunt Jemimas either. They *stuck to your ribs*.

After he *went to town*, Vancouver that is, he looked up his *skirt*. (No, he wasn't wearing a kilt or staring at girls on the bus. He visited his girlfriend.) He sometimes calls her his *old lady*, just as Dad called his Mother "the old lady." He calls *his* Mother Mom and his Dad is Dad. *The Old Man* is reserved for the "Bull", if he's a *pretty good head*.

He's decided the next time in town he'll bank some dough instead of blowing it on beer and clothes and then having to rely on *drag* from the *mancatcher* to get back. Luckily he knew he could get a loan from the logging firm's agent or he wouldn't have been able to get here in the first place. He'd probably be on the *skid road*. He has no desire to join those poor old *burned-out* loggers in the *flophouses* and at the *Sally Ann* putting in time till they go to the big logging camp in the sky. They're burned out because they always ate and ran, dosed their indigestion with generous amounts of baking soda, then they singed what was left of their stomachs with undiluted liquor.

10

A lot of them have *logger's small pox,* marks on their faces from a fight after somebody *took the boots to them,* stomped on them with their *cork* (caulk) boots, the ones with the nails on the bottom that keep a logger from falling from slippery logs.

He's not thinking about that anymore. It's almost *chow-time.* The cook's helper, *flunky* or *hasher,* is getting ready to beat that old *guthammer* (triangular piece of metal), with a hunk of iron. There's just time for a slug of *moose milk* (a deadly mixture of rum, milk and coffee—mostly rum) before taking on some more *grub.*

Wonder what's for supper?

Captain James Cook, the English explorer, first white man to "log" on our coast.

12

2.
Captain Cook
the logger.

Captain James Cook, the English explorer, is generally credited with being the first white man to "log" on the coast of what is now British Columbia.

Haida Indian war canoes.

There were, of course, "loggers" here long before Cook arrived in 1778. The Haida Indians, great warriors and travellers, fashioned huge cedar logs into canoes so they could go long distances to plunder tribes as far south as the Columbia River sandbars. Big trees in the Queen Charlotte Islands grew almost everywhere but some the Haidas chose were two or more miles from tidewater. To get them out of the forest they built log roads on which partially finished canoes were dragged to the sea, then floated to their villages where the canoes were further fashioned and made ready for the voyage.

13

Old chiefs told of slaves being used to drag out the logs with ropes made from hemlock roots. Remnants of the ancient roads they used are barely visible still, and modern day explorers report seeing abandoned canoes, forty feet long, upon which two hundred year old hemlocks are growing.

Captain Cook and the Haidas had this much in common: they were explorers and they needed the great trees to help them get where they were going.

According to Samwell's Journal, Cook entered Nootka Sound, on Vancouver Island's northwest coast, on March 29, 1778, seeking shelter and a place to cut trees to replace spars and masts broken during a rough voyage from New Zealand and the Sandwich Islands. (It was a lot rougher for Cook when he returned there later: the Hawaiians killed him.) At any rate, the natives here were friendly, so the cove was aptly named, Friendly Cove. The weather was extremely foggy, however, and an anchorage was carefully sought.

Portion of sketch by John Webber, Royal Navy, showing Captain Cook's ships the Resolution *and the* Discovery *in Nootka Sound in 1778.*

14

Although chronicler Samwell said, "as we were coming in we were surrounded by thirty or forty canoes full of Indians who expressed much astonishment at seeing the ship"; the Indians claimed they *sent out* two large canoes of braves which returned with "Captain Cook and his ship being towed behind them." The latter account appeared in the Ha-Shilth-Sa Indian newspaper and is based on stories reportedly handed down by tribal storytellers for more than two hundred years.

Mighty Nootka Chief Maquinna greeted Capt. Cook at Friendly Cove.

However Cook got into Friendly Cove, he landed safely and after establishing contact with the tribe, including famous Nootka Chief Maquinna, the ship's crew, in their quaint sailor uniforms and hats, strode ashore with broad axes and trimming tools to set about getting masts, spars and wood for the galley stoves. Here, and at Resolution Cove, they wooded, watered and "the people employed in striking the topmasts and unrigging them and the carpenters in caulking the ship's sides to make her as tight as we can against our Northern Expedition."

Friendly Cove, village of the Nootka Indians, as it was almost 200 years ago when English seacaptains sailed into the Nootka Sound region on Canada's Pacific Coast.

On Saturday, April 25, 1778, the Cook crew had completed their repairing of foremasts and shipping of a new mizzen mast and "likewise brewed beer enough to last the ship's company for three months." Captain Cook then headed out to sea and, for the purposes of this account, the first white "logger" sailed out of the picture.

He left behind a land where the trees were so huge they blotted out the sun. Few animals were seen within the damp canyons of green. In this rain forest, if birds sang at all, it was from branches that began hundreds of feet from the ground. The silence was broken by the wind and the seemingly endless rain which pounded the ground to a sodden mass.

The coast of the area that was to become British Columbia and Vancouver Island was literally one long forest stretching from waterline to mountaintop in an endless green belt. The islands dotting the sparkling green-blue sea was also covered with huge firs, cedars and arbutus where they were not studded with rock. It was a forbidding picture to most early visitors, including one who moaned: "I raised my eyes to the sky and could see nothing but the worthless timber that covered everything."

The forest stretched in one long line in an endless green belt.

15

The islands that dotted the sparkling green-blue sea were also covered with huge firs, cedars and arbutus where they were not studded with rock.

However useless they may have appeared to him, exploring and trading ships which followed Captain Cook also made use of the trees for ship repairs. And it wasn't long before farsighted merchants sitting in the comfort of their London offices saw the advantage of bringing home two cargoes for the price of one passage. Furs, the primary target for trade, took little space, so timbers in the rough could be decked and, after dressing in England, sold abroad.

Consequently, Captain John Meares received from his firm, Merchant Proprietors of London in December, 1787, the following instructions: "Spars of every denomination are constantly in demand here. Bring as many as you can conveniently stow." Soon the ship's carpenters were employed in cutting spars and sawing planks, particularly boats' knees and timbers, which brought a good price in China. When Meares left Nootka in September, 1788, the ship *Felice* was loaded and he was impressed: "Indeed the woods of this part of America are capable of supplying with their valuable materials, all the navies of Europe."

Captain John Meares. "Bring as many spars as you can conveniently stow."

The trading in spars and masts increased considerably as the spars became known for their strength. Tests were conducted at Portsmouth dockyard in December, 1847, to determine the comparative strength of the Vancouver Island Douglas Fir (named for Scottish botanist David Douglas who explored the Pacific Northwest in 1825) with what were called the "Riga spars", in use on British ships at that time. The tests showed that the Vancouver Island fir was superior to the Riga spar (named for the Baltic city from which they were shipped).

As a result of the test findings, the British Admiralty agreed to buy a cargo of spars for forty-five pounds for a sixty-two foot spar, twenty inches in diameter, and as high as one hundred pounds for a seventy-four foot spar, twenty-three inches in diameter. The contract was filled

"I raised my eyes to the sky and could see nothing but the worthless timber that covered everything."

17

by Captain Richard O. Hinderwell, who took with him aboard the *Albion*, Captain William Brotchie. Brotchie was reputed to know the coast well, having served aboard the Hudson's Bay Company's *Dryad*, but despite his navigational skills the *Albion* struck a reef situated off Victoria's Ogden Point. The reef has been known ever since as Brotchie's Ledge.

Early watercolor of Fort Victoria as it looked in 1854.

Sir James Douglas

18

Brotchie's misfortune continued as he then proceeded across the Strait of Juan de Fuca to anchor off New Dungeness, where *Albion's* crew felled trees and loaded spars from American territory. The Americans took a dim view of this, eventually. With a cargo worth about £3 thousand aboard, the *Albion* was seized by United States customs officials from Astoria, Washington, and the ship was subsequently sold. However, after a lengthy dispute that went all the way up the diplomatic channel to Washington, D.C., and involved the British Ambassador and the U.S. Treasury Department, the ship's owner, John Lidgett, was reimbursed the sum of $20 thousand. Lidgett got no ship back, of course, and the Admiralty got no spars.

Taking a break before loading the ship with lumber. Chemainus, 1902.

Undaunted, Brotchie, with his licence from the Hudson's Bay Company intact, went to Fort Rupert, at the northern end of Vancouver Island, and began to cut timber there. He used Indian labor and, according to a report by Captain Kuper (after whom a Gulf Island is named), the quality of the spars was "superior". But Brotchie had depleted all his resources and now had no way to get 107 spars to England. He appealed to Governor James Douglas who wrote to the Secretary of State for the

19

Fort Victoria, showing bastion. Fort built in 1843.

Colonies, pointing out that awarding a new spar contract to Brotchie would not only rescue a "worthy and enterprising man from ruin" but would give impulse to industry and the economy of the whole colony.

After several appeals from Douglas and others, during which time Brotchie went twice to San Francisco to try to dispose of the spars there, the British Admiralty finally declined to buy them. They told Governor Douglas that they had an ample supply in their dockyards. So far as is known, the spars never reached a market anywhere and Captain Brotchie, after a brief time as Harbormaster for Vancouver Island, died in Victoria on February 28, 1859, at the age of sixty.

Despite the setbacks suffered by Brotchie and the pessimism of the British Admiralty, lumbering flourished in the colony. Nonetheless, in the Guide to the Province of British Columbia for 1877-1878, T.N. Hibben & Co., Publishers, warned new arrivals that "logging and sawmilling will never be industries much relied upon by newly arrived emigrants from Europe as the various descriptions of labor required are best carried on by persons who have had special training."

The old Hudson's Bay Company's building inside the fort.

Canadian Puget Sound Lumber & Timber Company located on tidewater on Upper Harbor, Victoria.

20

Two early loggers stand on "springboards" which they have inserted in the tree and from which they make their undercut.

Early loggers hewing timbers on the spot in the woods. Notice peaveys, and man in centre of photo wields broad-bladed "Hudson's Bay" axe.

21

A total of 366 billion board feet of merchantable timber in 1921. White spruce stand.

The Guide did not say how the newcomer was to gain this special training but wisely noted that the "settler who is near any main line of communication should not look upon his fine timber as a valueless possession which may be wasted improvidently. The timber on his farm may, within his own lifetime, be worth as much as the soil of his farm."

That statement would be made from time to time throughout the history of logging in British Columbia.

By the end of 1870, the logging industry was well on its way, and during the ten years up to that time about 60 million feet of rough and dressed Douglas fir lumber, with a quantity of shingles, laths, pickets and about 3,500 spars were exported.

Wages to woodsmen ranged from twenty-five to forty-five gold dollars a month for "a few of the more skilled and responsible men."

Much later, in 1921, the Handbook of the Legislative Assembly was boasting that the "one and most readily available and most important of British Columbia's natural resources is her immense timber reserve." Recent statistics, it reported, gave the Province approximately 366 billion board feet of merchantable timber with important commercial species being Douglas fir, Western red cedar, silver spruce, Western soft pine, Western hemlock, Engelmann spruce, cottonwood and balsam.

"The most readily available and most important of British Columbia's natural resources is her immense timber reserve."

This old beauty is on view at British Columbia Forest Museum near Duncan.

Douglas firs up to 300 feet high and with a base circumference of thirty to forty feet were attainable from the Rockies to the coast. Western cedar averaged 125 feet with diameters of four to eight feet, "sometimes growing to a height of 200 feet and a diameter of fourteen to eighteen feet."

Obviously, in 1921, a long time after Captain Cook, the British Columbia logging industry—number one in the Province—still had only one way to go: up.

By 1921 no one was complaining about not being able to see the sky for trees.

23

Moodyville Sawmill, Moodyville, B.C. The date of the photo is not known except that it appeared in a pamphlet "British Columbia's Supreme Advantage in Climate, Resources, Beauty and Life" by Moses B. Cotsworth, F.G.S. and published by the B.C. Government in 1909.

3.
Milling Around B.C.
From 1848 to Hillcrest.

"Spars from the North American shores of the Pacific will always command a high price in Spain, France, and England," wrote Matthew MacFie in May, 1865.

You would think that MacFie, Fellow of the Royal Geographic Society and "five years a resident of Victoria," had never heard of Captain Brotchie, but by 1865 the colony's sawmilling industry had gone through several boom and bust periods, a condition persisting to this day. Viewed in the light of that knowledge, MacFie's statement becomes more understandable.

The first sawmill in what was to become British Columbia was built by the Hudson's Bay Company near Victoria. Machine-operated, the water-powered mill at Millstream began operations on November 24, 1848. Millstream was a freshwater brook at the head of Esquimalt Harbor, one-quarter of a mile above the present Parson's Bridge, six miles west of Victoria.

Millstream mill had a varied career and a doubtful future from the start. Plagued by a lack of water during dry seasons and dry years, it was also endangered by too much water. In 1854 or 1855, a freshet washed out the waterwheel and seriously damaged both the sawmill and the gristmill erected beside it. It closed down, although the waterwheel had been replaced and the mill started operations again for a short time.

On April 27, 1849, in its heyday, a shipment of lumber was sent from the Millstream mill to Langley, a Hudson's Bay Company outpost on an arm of the lower Fraser River, the first lumber to be sent from Vancouver Island, as far as records show. The mill was also the first in the colony to enter the export trade and shipped more than 42 thousand feet of lumber to San Francisco during the California Gold Rush.

25

At Sooke, also on Vancouver Island, Captain W.C. Grant built a sawmill which he soon sold to John Muir & Sons in 1853. It was moved within the mouth of Sooke Harbor and converted to steam in 1855. Destroyed by fire twenty years later, it was rebuilt three years after that, and remained in operation until 1892.

Coal mining on Vancouver Island was also becoming an important industry and a great deal of lumber was required for pit props and other mine construction. A water-power mill completed at Nanaimo in October, 1854, was the second Hudson's Bay Company mill on the island and was built partially to fulfill the developing industry's needs. Located about six hundred yards from the original Bastion in the Hub City, the new mill stood on the banks of the Salt Spring River.

Left: John Muir and Sons sawmill at Sooke on Vancouver Island. Built in 1849 by Captain W.C. Grant who sold it to Muir in 1853. It was moved from within harbor to mouth of harbor and converted to steam in 1855.

Right: General view of Nanaimo and the Hudsons Bay Fort as it looked in 1868.

Oxen brought from Victoria hauled the logs for the mill's output, most of them supplied by the Nanaimo Indians. According to an old report the saw logs had to be no less than fifteen inches in diameter at the small end and fifteen feet long. Delivery price was nominal, even for those times: one Hudson's Bay blanket for every eight logs. The thrifty millers also cut the price if the logs weren't long enough. The occasional undersized shipment was purchased at a reduced tariff of sixteen for a blanket.

This scene shows the entire logging crew at D.B. Charleson's camp near Fraser Mills in 1890. Note the well worn skid road. The bull-puncher will be the man with the prod at the rear of the bulls.

26

The first mill on the British Columbia mainland, New Caledonia as it was then known, was built in 1858 by Land, Fleming & Company at Fort Yale on the Fraser River. Gold miners had arrived a year earlier and the peaceful fur-trading community was soon converted to a tent town filled with 5,000 brawling residents who wanted places to live and to spend their money. Land & Fleming soon moved their mill from its original location to a site south of the town and began producing 6,000 feet of lumber daily, most of it slated for construction at the townsite. The price was $125 a thousand board feet.

In 1860, one of New Westminster's pioneer residents, H.A.R. Homer, started a mill in the Royal City. As well as operating the steam-powered mill on the North Arm of the Fraser River, a little below the early city, Homer also owned a lumberyard in the city.

Although conditions appeared rosy with new mills springing up and an air of seeming prosperity in the lumber industry, the colony's first decade of sawmilling ended on a note of uncertainty. Manufactured lumber from the United States was being imported at an increasing rate; it must have seemed strange to the colonists to see lumber being imported into a country largely covered by trees. As MacFie said five years later: "Unless wealthy and enterprising companies enter briskly into this sort of (lumber) exportation, it is hardly necessary to say that the balance of trade will be increasingly against the colony."

Early view of Yale with the steamship, paddlewheeler Rithet which brought people and supplies up to the community on the Fraser River. During Gold Rush Yale supported five thousand souls and required vast amounts of lumber from first mill on Mainland established at Yale by Land, Fleming and Company.

Ox teams at Yale, B.C.—starting point of the Cariboo Road.

Royal City Planing Mills, southend Carrall Street on False Creek, under construction at time of the great fire on June 13, 1886. This lumberyard was used as collecting point for bodies of those who lost their lives in the fire. Building on left is office and was, for a few days, used as Post Office for Vancouver. R.C. Ferguson was mill manager.

27

Captain Edward Stamp, pioneer sawmill operator. He quarrelled with others in Hastings Mill, sold out, and went to England in 1872 to raise money for another venture. Died there that year.

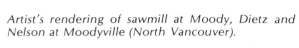

Artist's rendering of sawmill at Moody, Dietz and Nelson at Moodyville (North Vancouver).

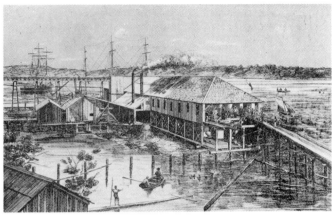

The explanation for this lack of expansion in the late 1850s could well have been the effect of an economic depression which arrived about 1857. There was insufficient capital—despite the Fraser River Gold Rush—for the construction of new mills; there was also a shortage of labor. During the first half of the next decade, however, lumber production was stimulated somewhat and a number of new mills opened both on Vancouver Island and on the Mainland.

One, the famous Anderson and Anderson Mill at Port Alberni, built in 1861, was referred to as "Stamp's Mill" after Captain Edward Stamp, shipmaster in their employ. It was equipped with six gang of saws and by August that year was producing 14,000 feet of lumber daily. A month earlier it had commenced shipping its products to Peru and Australia.

Another sawmill of that era is worthy of mention: The Shepard Mill located on the Shawnigan River near Mill Bay, Vancouver Island, was sold to W.P. Sayward, the owner of a lumberyard, who entered the export trade with shipments of lumber to San Francisco. The mill continued to operate until 1890 when a new mill was established in Victoria. This new mill became the Canadian Puget Sound Lumber & Timber Co. Ltd.

Whenever the economy sagged in early British Columbia, someone would come along and shout: "Gold!" After that things would usually pick up again. Gold on the Fraser. Gold in the Cariboo. Gold in the Klondike.

28

Georgia Street log that was part of huge fir that fell during storm in 1886. Tree was at corner of Georgia and Granville and was 14 feet at the stump. Remnants were widely displayed in Eastern Canada.

Barkerville, the mining town on Williams Creek, just before the fire of 1868.

29

Loading ships at Moodyville (north Vancouver) showing Mirzapore in fore-ground. About 1888.

The wave of prosperity which swept the country as a result of the discovery and yield from the rich diggings in the Cariboo created a heavy demand for lumber, especially in Victoria, where it was needed for everything from building more saloons to construction of sidewalks over the city's many mud holes. The Island city, destined to become capital of the Province of British Columbia, was then the jumping off spot for many miners and the community spread arms in all directions to embrace these adventurers. Both Island and Mainland mills met part of these lumber requirements and, as time went by, gradually supplanted shipments from the Puget Sound mills in United States. Although exports continued throughout the decade, progress in the colony itself was slow. The wave of prosperity was short-lived, turning into a severe slump from which the economy did not fully recover until 1879.

Even so, mill construction was not halted. In 1863, New Westminster's second mill, the British Columbia Mill Company, was built on the river front with berthing facilities for ships and equipped to manufacture flooring as well as other dressed items. At the same time, Pioneer Mills at Moodyville, the future North Vancouver City, on the north shore of Burrard Inlet was started. It failed in six months and was taken over by John Smith who changed its name to Burrard Inlet Mills. Under this name the first lumber shipment to leave mainland British Columbia for an overseas market was loaded on the barque *Ellen Lewis* for shipment on November 9, 1864. Part of the cargo was from New Westminster and it cleared there, bound for Australia.

Whipsawing lumber at Dease River, near Cassiar in northern B.C. Reason for ghostly image on top man with saw was shaft of light that came through trees at that point. Photo was retouched by Barbara Davies of B.C. Forest Service.

Early Victoria, this shot taken from Douglas Street looking west along Johnson Street.

That same year, 1864, T.G. Askew opened a mill at Chemainus on Vancouver Island. The mill was sold in 1880 by Askew's widow to Croft & Severn, although the latter partner sold his interest in 1887 when the mill became known as the Croft and Argus mill. Croft was a son-in-law of Robert Dunsmuir, the coal baron, owner of the Esquimalt & Nanaimo Railway, who soon became the mill's best customer. Argus was also railroad-connected; he was the brother of R.B. Argus, vice-president of the Canadian Pacific Railroad.

Georgia Street log which fell during storm in Vancouver at Georgia and Granville Streets. Centre man is Sam Brighouse. End man on right is Jack Fannin and man with white hair is Captain Powers of Moodyville Hotel. Others are unidentified in this photo taken in 1886.

Moodyville, or Moody's Mills, after 1864. Barque Ellen Lewis, first ship, departed Nov. 9, 1864 with lumber for Australia. Employees' homes on hill. Note ease of logging. Fallers cut trees which, when bucked, were rolled right into Inlet.

The mill supplied all the lumber for the railway's construction, some 12 million feet, as well as most of the lumber used on the east coast of Vancouver Island. Croft and Argus owned the Chemainus townsite and large timber lands on the Island as well as on the Mainland. However, the year 1889 saw the mill in the hands of J.S. Humbird, an American, who, with Dunsmuir, formed the Victoria Lumber and Manufacturing Company. They built a new mill near the site of the original Askew Mill which is still in operation today; since 1944 it has been known as Chemainus Division of MacMillan Bloedel.

In 1867, the year of Confederation in other parts of the country (British Columbia joined in 1870), the provincial forest industry really got into stride. It was the year for the largest amount of lumber exported to that time: 20 million board feet. It also was the year that production began at "Hastings Mill", which, like the Anderson and Anderson Mill at Port Alberni, was also known as "Stamp's Mill", after Captain Stamp. There had been much indecision at the time about where this mill should be located and finally it was decided it should be erected on a point of land projecting halfway between what is now Stanley Park and the end of New Road, now Hastings Street. Around this mill grew the present city of Vancouver. During its long operating career, 1867 to 1928, Hastings Mill contributed much to the establishment of the lumbering industry in British Columbia. As well as loading large cargoes for export, Captain Stamp also entered briskly into the local market and into competition with Moody's Mill and the B.C. Mill, at Moodyville and New Westminster. The first part of 1868 saw fourteen vessels loaded with the company's lumber and shingles. Two thousand spars were shipped, too. The spars were reported to have been as long as 150 feet and "free from knots."

Towards the end of the 1860s the Vancouver harbor became site of a new forest: this one was of masts. In 1869, twenty-one ships were loaded at Stamp's Hastings Mill and twenty-four cleared the Moodyville Mill, making the harbor a very busy place. Eighty per cent of these cargoes went to South America, Australia and San Francisco, with twenty per cent going to China, England and the Hawaiian Islands. Meantime, Captain Stamp was busy doing more than shipping lumber. He was acquiring large tracts of the best timberland in the area and that is one of the reasons the Hastings Mill lasted as long as it did. Stamp took advantage of the Land Ordinance of 1865 which authorized forest land to be sold at one dollar an acre. It was under this law that Stamp purchased nearly all the timberland between New Westminster and Point Grey and all the timberland from Point Grey to False Creek. He also had access to all the good timberland on Howe Sound.

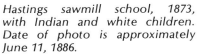

Hastings sawmill school, 1873, with Indian and white children. Date of photo is approximately June 11, 1886.

Hastings Sawmill, Burrard Inlet, copied from very old photograph, 1883 or earlier.

Duke and Duchess of Cornwall and York being received at Hastings Mill, September 30, 1901. Sir Wilfred Laurier on edge of carpet. Note mounted horse guard.

Georgia Street fir that fell during storm onto what is now Vancouver's entertainment district. The butt measured over 14 feet across and was cut up in sections for display at exhibitions in Toronto and London.

Filing room men prepare to replace a dulled saw with a freshly sharpened one at Saltaire Lumber in Ladysmith.

On January 2, 1869, Stamp retired from the management of the company's affairs due to a quarrel with his partners and Captain J.A. Raymur succeeded him. In 1870 the mill was sold to J.C. Nicholson on behalf of Dickson, DeWolfe & Co. of San Francisco who changed the name to Hastings Sawmill Company. Ownership changed again in 1889 to John Hendry, president and general manager of New Westminster City Planing Mills Company. The two companies then merged to become the B.C. Mills Timber and Trading Co. Ltd., with Hendry as president, and the mill itself was enlarged. By 1890 the business had a foreign and local trade of 250 thousand feet per day. The plant continued until 1928 when the mill site was purchased by the Federal Harbors Board.

Taking a rest for the photographer were these early loggers (bullpuncher standing). Taken after July, 1890. The turn of logs were on their way to the saw-mill at Millside, future Fraser Mills, from camp owned by Ross, McLaren, owners. Note the biggest log is in front to jerk smaller logs behind.

Canadian Western Lumber Co. Ltd. townsite, best known as "Fraser Mills." The houses, built for French-speaking workers brought from Quebec, have all been removed. Fraser Mills is now operated by Crown Zellerbach.

Logs entering Fraser Mills, or Canadian Western Lumber Co. Ltd., as it was then known.

One of the largest and most up-to-date lumbering operations for its time came haltingly into existence at Millside on the Fraser River, below what is now the area known as Maillardville, named for a young French Oblate community worker. It was at this site in January, 1889, that Ross, McLaren Sawmills of Vancouver began plant construction for what was to become the largest sawmill operation in the world at that time. It was a major project costing some $350,000, a large amount for those days.

The site was in a wild state, in more than one way. In fact, the whole of the Municipality of Coquitlam was running wild. A newspaper of the day reported that deer, bear, mink, raccoons, wild cats, muskrats and other "predators" roamed free. The Municipal Council found it expedient to pass bounties on these animals, with bears bringing two dollars and fifty cents for their hides while mink were worth twenty five cents and bluejays three cents apiece. Despite the wilderness conditions, on September 15, 1890, the *Columbian* newspaper reported that a row of houses was being built at Millside, the little railroad junction on the branch line from Westminster Junction. The Ross, McLaren mill whistle was blown for the first time and could be heard approximately three miles away. Its replacement many years later could be heard on a clear day as far away as White Rock and might be heard still except environmentalists recently objected to its "noise pollution" so it was silenced.

While the year 1890 might have been a good year for blowing whistles, company executives found it an exceedingly bad year for selling lumber. To add to market problems, sparkplug president James McLaren died. Things got even worse in 1893: the weather was disastrous.

Carrall Street looking south from corner of Water Street in "Gastown," Vancouver. Under the famous Maple Tree, candidates to first civic election spoke to the few residents who would listen. Indian name for site was LuckLucky. Here "Gassy Jack," the pioneer taverner who gave Gastown its name, built in 1867.

On February 1 the Fraser River froze completely across, disrupting shipping, and skating was the only business of the day. The Millside mill remained silent and in February of 1899 the timber limits of Ross, McLaren Company on Vancouver Island were put up for sale. The mill was finally re-opened after it had been idle for almost ten years. At least, news of the mill's re-opening was announced on March 10, 1903. The new company was to be known as Fraser River Sawmills, but installation of new machinery and procrastination over improvements to the river channel stymied progress again. It wasn't until January, 1906, that a German barque finished loading lumber for Australia and became the first ship to take a cargo from the docks for the new company.

Old waterpower mill located on the North Thompson River.

On September 3, 1907, a syndicate headed by A.D. McRae of Winnipeg and Peter Jansen of Nebraska invested in Fraser River Sawmills. It was reported by the *Columbian* newspaper that $2.5 million was involved in a transfer of controlling interest. But it was not a good year for investment. Dunn's Business analysts announced that the lumbering business in British Columbia was in a depressed state, one of the reasons being tariffs. During 1907 Canada imported from United States, free of incoming duty, nearly $8 million worth of lumber while sales to that country amounted to very little, and even on these there was applied a two dollar levy on every thousand feet. The industry for the whole of Canada employed only between 65,000 and 75,000 men and the average wage dropped from thirty five dollars to twenty five dollars a month. Total production for the whole country was less than 100,000 feet.

37

Crow's Nest Pass Lumber Company at Galloway, B.C.

Waterpowered Georgetown Sawmill. Originally built in 1875 by James Brown on Indian land near Prince Rupert. Logs cut by Indians. Brown, a white man, married Indian princess. Mill ran until fairly recently. Notice water barrels on roofs. Photo was taken in 1914 for British Columbia Forest Service by early Chief Forester, M. Allerdale Grainger.

In 1910 the Canadian Western Lumber Company took over the charter of Fraser River Lumber Company. It remained in the same hands for many years and continually expanded. The company's major interest was acquired in 1953 by Crown Zellerbach. Fraser Mills (it is still known as that today), employed 877 employees in 1913. They were "mostly French-Canadian and European", also fifty-seven Japanese, twenty-nine Chinese and 168 East Indians. The predominance of French-speaking Canadians came about in 1909 when a nightwatchman named Theroux and a Reverend Father O'Boyle were dispatched to Quebec to recruit labor from the lumber camps there. According to a history of Maillardville and Fraser Mills this quest was due to "dissatisfaction with Oriental labor." Whatever the reason, on September

Waterpowered Brown's Mill, 35 miles from Prince Rupert up the Exstall tributary of the Skeena River. On an island, it was built in 1903 by James Brown who also built the famous Georgetown Mill in 1875. One of the few waterpowered mills still in existence in B.C. Brown's Mill is operated by a descendent of Brown, James Donaldson, on a part-time basis.

28, 1909, the first contingent of 110 French-speaking workers arrived by special Canadian Pacific Railway train. The mill company had set aside land in one acre lots for them to build on; some houses were already standing and a new hotel was ready to accommodate 300 people. A second Quebec migration came in 1910.

39

Miller Lumber Carrier in operation at Fraser Mills, circa 1925.

Sawmill at old Fort George, 1910. The area was destined to become Prince George, today still site for sawmills and pulpmills.

Mill yard at Sinclair and Schultz at Atlin, B.C. near Yukon border.

Ron Round, personnel manager at Fraser Mills, started there in 1933 at sixteen, packing lumber on his shoulder for twenty five cents an hour. He was glad to get the job in the Depression, having been chosen with two others out of a crowd of about one hundred men waiting outside the office.

40

Whipsawing at Finlay Junction, Fort George area, 1914. Man on top of saw followed mark. Next to pushing and pulling, man on bottom's biggest problem was keeping sawdust out of eyes. Capacity, 150 running feet a day.

"In those days you pleased the foreman who was God in his own department," Round said. "Of course, it had advantages. If you were fired, you just walked into another department and got another job." Wages were set "at the whim of the foreman."

As many as 120 men were engaged in piling lumber, a job now done at the same mill by one fork lift truck. Mr. Round recalls that the mill was not the safest place to work in those days but people were "more rough and ready and didn't worry about a few scratches." Like the man who cut three fingers off in a planer and then refused a ride, preferring to walk to the first aid station a quarter of a mile away. That was the same man that Round saw one day filing his teeth with a large Bastard file!

There was no mobile equipment in the mill in 1933. A huge barn held the horsepower, about one hundred of them. These Clydesdale hay-burners lived, worked and died within the confines of the millsite. The same could be said for some of the Chinese and East Indian workers. Inside the millsite were "Chinatown" and "Hindu Town" and both were the subject of much amusement and interest to white workers.

41

Taking out logs by locie at Hillcrest Lumber Company, Mesachie Lake, 18 miles west of Duncan on old Lake Cowichan Road.

Portable sawmill (believed to be that of Simon Konacher) similar to many bush mills using horses and half a dozen men in whole operation. This mill also has edger.

42

"At lunchtime we used to tear over to Lim Sing's store to play fantan," Round said. Workers also drank beer and stole chocolate bars. Indulgent Lim Sing didn't bat an eyelash because he was taking in a good profit on the games. "Some of our company managers of today stole bars from that store," said Maurice Thomas, now sawmill superintendent.

The East Indian community within the mill was even more fascinating because at that time Hindus were cremated on the shores of the Fraser River and the ashes deposited with ceremony in the water.

"We always knew when there was going to be a cremation," Thomas said. "The East Indian workers used to collect the slabs and planer ends to use for the fire." He and other workers would hide and watch the ritual.

Another source of amusement was to catch the boommen supposedly working on the river trying to sneak through the woods at night to grab a quick beer a Lim Sing's. "They never knew how we caught them at it," Thomas Said. "They had lamps on their hats, something like miner's. And you could see them moving and know where they were headed."

Maurice Thomas started as a boomman in 1938. His father, John Thomas, came from Quebec in 1908. The senior Thomas ran a mule team delivering groceries from the company store. He became foreman on the logs and worked till seventy, the latter years on the hog fuel scows.

"He was mad at having to retire," his son said. "He used to say he'd go get a job in a logging camp."

Fraser Mills was a colorful place to work and live, mainly because of a feeling of "family". Trees had been planted on both sides of the main street, King Edward Avenue, and townsite residents enjoyed frequent social gatherings, including square dances and parties. The top storey of the store served as a community hall and wives and daughters of company officials joined in helping plan festive occasions.

"The general store was the centre of the community," Round said. "You could buy anything you wanted as long as you had coupons. At the end of the month some people's cheques were only for a dollar or fifty cents because they'd couponed themselves to death at the store." He recalled going there once to cash in two dollars worth of coupons so he could take his date to a movie.

The main street was liveliest during shift changes when the interurban tram came in from New Westminster with workers "hanging on the sides like flies." The millsite had its own constable who patrolled the beat on foot and horseback. One day he was demonstrating his favorite possession, his gun. It was for a practical purpose: to try to scare a drunk into foresaking forever the evils of liquor. Unfortunately the gun went off and the constable shot himself through the foot.

The "family" environment has changed at Fraser Mills now. Crown Zellerbach runs it as an efficient operation, although descendents of the early workers still punch time cards and eat in modern lunchrooms. The last old houses on King Edward Avenue were removed from their

Hillcrest Lumber Company at Mesachie Lake, just after it closed in 1969. At its peak mill employed 400 and could handle anything from big timber to mouldings.

Loading railway sleepers on trucks for creosoting, 1914. Early mills employed many husky East Indians for heavy work. Many still work at sawmills in province.

44

boggy setting when the Port Mann Freeway was built, but, along with its colorful past, Fraser Mills still lives.

Another interesting story, but one without as happy an ending, is that of Hillcrest Lumber Company Ltd. Owned by the Stone family, Hillcrest employed about 400 workers, including those in the mill, power plant and in the woods. Located on Mesachie Lake, eighteen miles west of Duncan, the mill ran fir, cedar, hemlock and pine. Anything they got an order for they cut; from the biggest timber right down to fine mouldings. Eventually, however, Hillcrest ran out of timber because the company didn't hold any large leases and couldn't afford to truck in logs when their own nearby stands ran out. They decided in 1969 to "close 'er down." The company turned over its sewer and water system in the community to Cowichan Valley Regional District for the legal minimum of one dollar. The mill was dismantled and the equipment carted off to other mills. The site was razed and the land sold.

Most of the workers who had been there for up to twenty five years were relocated by Canada Manpower; others refused to move or were too old and loyal to the community. The seventy or so company-owned houses soon filled up with workers at other sites in the Lake Cowichan-Honeymoon Bay area.

One of those who refused to leave was Wilbur Lee, watchman. "It was a good outfit to work for," Lee said. There was only one major hassle between company and labor—IWA and Operating Engineers—and that was over curtailment of bus services.

"The company held onto its employees," Lee said. "They even gave us a turkey every Christmas. Not many firms do that any more. And the wives of the bosses—they talked to you just like anybody else.

"Some people cried when they shut this place down."

Steam cold decker at Old Hillcrest, 1937.

H.S. Rowling's logging camp on the McMillan farm in Surrey in 1896. Note that the logs have already been peeled and bucked and now the bullpuncher is getting ready to herd the bulls into position for hauling the logs out.

46

4.
Men And Other Beasts of Burden

The bulls, horses, donkeys and cats.

It is a crisp and clear day on this morning in 1880, a rare, rainless day in the forest of British Columbia. Or what is to be British Columbia.

Two men suddenly leap back from the huge fir tree they have been hacking at with their single-bitted axes with strange curved heads. The tree gives a strangled cry like a human in agony, wavers on its bleeding six foot stump for a long moment, then begins to fall, complaining loudly, through the outstretched, breaking limbs of its forest mates. It shudders for a moment on the forest floor before settling into its bruised bark and broken branches.

The "Fallers" have been watching this death of the ancient fir in silence. Now they shoulder their axes and saws and head for another tree. Other men enter the scene. "Buckers" these are, come to cut the tree into logs which are already being limbed and peeled by "Barkers." "Snipers" shape the butt ends of the logs so they look a little like sharpened pencils or huge sled runners.

A "Dogger" drives large steel eyelets called "dogs" into each log so chains can be passed through to link the huge logs together.

Now a most important gentleman appears. He is in charge of teams of oxen, called "bulls". He is the "Bull Puncher", possessor of an impressive vocabulary made up of profane and abusive words, the most feared and respected man in the woods. It is his job to keep the bulls working, to orchestrate, choreograph and set the tone for this whole logging "show." In addition to his loud voice and choice language, the bull puncher is distinctive because of his "goad", a sharp rod used to prod the bulls into action. The goad is more than a work implement, however. It is the mark of a man of superior bearing, a symbol that he may

47

carry off the job, just as other men of refinement carry canes or batons. An early description of the bull puncher noted that he was a "celebrity" and "usually Scotch or of Scotch descent, rugged, honest and drinker of plenty of hard liquor." The bullpuncher now positions his animals in front of the logs about to be transported to the water's edge where they can be floated down to the mill for cutting into lumber.

The way has already been prepared. A "skid road" lies like a crude railway line—with ties but no rails—all the way down to the water. The men responsible for this road are the "Swampers" who cleared the bush and stumps off the roadway. "Skidders" came along and imbedded short hemlock logs crosswise at regular intervals. A "Greaser" has smeared these logs with whale oil or crude oil to make them easier for the bulls to pull the logs over. The skid road has been well planned and built with precision because the logs must not bump on the cross logs and must keep fairly close to the centre on curves.

The bullpuncher is now ready to move and he yells: "Giddap!" and "Hiiyaaahh!", startling the birds and small woodland creatures into flight. This initial yell is but a warning and is followed by a string of crudity that immediately brings looks of envy from lesser mortals in this tableau. Yoked and chained together, the big bulls tug and strain at the huge logs, the men helping them get started by rolling and pushing at the timber with cant hooks—forerunners of the "peavey" except that they have blunt ends—and pinch bars, levers with pointed projections at one end, rather like crow bars.

At the end of the "turn" of logs is attached a small hollow log containing an axe, a sledge hammer and, perhaps, some "dogs". It also contains the "Pig Man", for this hollowed log is called the "pig." It will be uncoupled at the water's edge by the Pig Man who will collect the dogs after they have been removed by the doggers, then the pig will be attached to the bulls to return with them to the woods. This time, however, the Pig Man does not ride. He is a low individual, far down the social scale. No . . . the pig on its return will be ridden by the bullpuncher, that prince among men.

The bullpuncher and his crew worked hard for ten hours every day and any comfort they got was well earned. It wasn't any easier for the animals. From 1860 nearly to the turn of the century, they were the mainstay of logging transportation, and were sometimes killed in the line of duty.

Jack Scott, a successful Hornby Island logger, used a string of ten oxen to bring out logs until a tree fell on them and killed them. (In the early 1900s, Scott drove his last team of oxen through the streets of Nanaimo.) It was an ignominious fate that awaited the poor accident victim. He ended up in the stew pot, or as roasts, welcomed by loggers who had existed on a steady diet of salt pork, beans, flapjacks and stewed prunes. But with no meat tenderizer, the bull's meat was often tough. As one old logger reported, "the loudest cuss ever heard in a bunkhouse was when a logger bit into a yoke buckle on his roast beef!"

The bulls were not mistreated. Off duty they were kept in cedar shake-roofed barns, open at the sides, which kept off some of the elements. And, as with later, man-made equipment, they were serviced in order to be in shape for the heavy work. In large logging operations, one or

Oxen had to be shod because tender feet would get sore at the end of the day hauling logs.

Although the bulls were well cared for in most cases, some still were killed on the job and the victims frequently became part of the fare at the loggers' table—which must have led to mixed emotions.

A 1919 skid road using roader donkey with the Pig Man riding the "pig" at the end of the turn of logs. Note that he is carrying his axe and peavey in the hollowed out log. Oxen-pulled logs had same set-up.

Once at the landing the logs are unchained and the "dogs" removed for use on the next "turn" of logs. Note the "boom" of beautiful logs sorted and ready to be moved to the mill.

49

two blacksmiths were retained to shoe the animals, two plates on each cloven hoof. While oxen used on farms did not require shoes because the soil was soft underfoot, in the woods they tramped all day over fallen logs, debris and the skid roads. Under such rough conditions their shoes sometimes broke or fell off and had to be replaced. A stall-like frame was built near the log dump where the bull was unhitched, led into the frame, his head secured in a stanchion so he was unable to move. A heavy canvas or ox hide belt attached to one side of the stall was passed under his belly. The end was fastened to a windlass, a horizontal barrel turned by a crank, which was wound up, lifting the bull off his feet so his hooves could be shod.

A logging camp in the forest, now Kitsilano, Vancouver, in 1890. The logs were yarded to a logging railway, reputed to have been the first in B.C. operated by steam, by sixteen oxen. Logs were loaded on cars and hauled on iron rails to a log dump on shore of English Bay at the foot of Trutch Street. They were there boomed and towed to Hastings Mill.

The bulls were not branded like their beefy cousins on the range but, surprisingly, there are no accounts of rustling among the logging firms.

Much of the early bull-team logging was done on the homesteads of the pioneers. One such pioneer was Grant Garnett, interviewed at his Victoria home when he was ninety-two years old.

Garnett's father, Frank Garnett, brought his family to Mill Bay to log and farm two hundred acres after his shingle mill, built in 1889, at Oyster Bay near Ladysmith, burned down. Like his father, born of Irish stock near London, Ontario, Grant Garnett worked ten hours a day from the time he was thirteen so the land could be cleared for farming. They were assisted by a crew of Chinese hired in Victoria for ninety cents a day. "Overalls cost a dollar ten a pair and six tins of snoose were a buck and a quarter," Garnett said. "You couldn't log without snoose."

This historic photo was of the largest log taken out of Maple Bay at the turn of century. Shown are bull-puncher Jim Norris (on wagon), Frank Garnett, owner (left); Minnie Frayne with Myrtle; Tom P. Barry, holding eldest daughter, Adelaide; Lettie, his wife, and Mrs. Frank Garnett. Garnett was killed shortly afterward taking out the last turn of logs on his property. He got wedged between two logs and crushed.

Ironically, the senior Garnett was taking his final turn of logs off the property when he became wedged between two of them and bled to death at the scene.

"My poor old mother stayed there for two hours and waited until he died," Garnett said. "He kept asking for her to hit him on the head with the sledge hammer, but she wouldn't do it. She died herself not long after that."

Horses such as these magnificent beasts replaced the bulls, or oxen, as the mainstay of the logging operations in British Columbia. Horses were smarter, stronger and had prettier ears—see how these are all standing straight up.

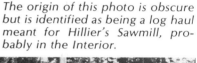

The origin of this photo is obscure but is identified as being a log haul meant for Hillier's Sawmill, probably in the Interior.

Horse logging in the winter time at Aleza Lake Mills.

Bonner's Ferry Lumber Co. near Cranbrook, horse logging on January 1, 1913.

The Garnetts cut and hauled to the mill the largest fir ever cut at Mill Bay and also experimented with the use of both horses and bulls on the same string. Horses were found to be better pullers and more agile in the woods and gradually they became standard equipment all over British Columbia. Moodyville Mill also tried a string of ten mules, but mules—a hybrid combination of horse and donkey—never became popular as a logging beast.

The bulls were still around till after 1900. Meanwhile, men wrestled with logs in many ways to get them to the mill. Once in the water they were "boomed up" and moved to a "pool" where they remained until time for a log drive.

Wagon train hauling lumber for a flume at Walhachin, historic town between Cache Creek and Kamloops. Circa 1910.

Putting the undercut in a huge red cedar. The fallers take it easy for this gag shot possibly taken at Myrtle Point in 1924. Fallers stood on springboards sometimes as much as six and eight feet above the ground.

Leamy and Kyle Sawmill on False Creek, Vancouver, in 1890. Cassidy and Company took over in 1897. Mill closed in 1899. This scene is from a spot looking east from the foot of Ash Street.

52

Loggers on Lake Cowichan on Vancouver Island had to drive their logs down the Cowichan River to the sea. The river was filled with falls and rapids with drops of ten feet and more. The water level had to be judged carefully. If it was too high the logs floated onto flats where they would lie and rot. If the river was too low the logs jammed and piled up like matchsticks. In the early days Indians helped on log drives, paddling in and out in their canoes, preventing snagging and jamming and helping dislodge logs from the banks. If the jams were too big for men to move, dynamite charges were placed in the confusion of timber.

Loggers on the Upper Fraser piled their products along the banks until the ice went out when they would be floated to the mills, while men in boats kept them clear of snags and hangups. This type of drive was at its peak in 1930.

Horse logging in the heart of the city, or what was to become the corner of Kingsway and Gilley in Burnaby. Note logs on skidroad and planks covering culvert crossing the main road. Wagon driver patiently awaits his turn to cross busy intersection.

The locality of this photograph is not known but is believed to have been the north arm of Burrard Inlet or near Gibson's Landing, now Gibson's, B.C. Stables on left indicate bulls, mules or horses were used. Buildings made of split cedar shakes. Logs came down hillside on log chutes with terrific speed and force. Sometimes they sped so fast they were burning when they hit the water.

53

The highest paid and most dangerous profession was that of the highrigger, shown here topping a big fir at A.&L. Logging Company, Camp 3, 1926. The big tree became the centre of the logging operation, all the other trees being yarded into here by the donkey engine for shipment out to the mill.

But the time came when getting logs meant going farther and farther into the woods. It became necessary to devise some means to gather fallen trees in a central location and this is when the spar tree became part of the logging scene. Specially chosen trees were limbed and topped by adventurous, highly skilled men called "High Riggers" who were equipped with a special belt, spiked climbing spurs strapped to their boots, a small axe and a one-man crosscut saw. High riggers wore lifelines made of manila with a wire core. It was strong but not so strong that they couldn't cut through it quickly, for example, if a tree should split after being topped.

The prepared spar tree now became the focal point of the logging operation. Something was required to "yard" the logs into this area. "Power yarding" was first used in the Pacific Northwest about 1890. The machine involved was a fairly simple affair, consisting of a vertical windlass and a vertical engine attached to an upright boiler. The windlass, or spool, was driven directly by a pinion wheel and was mounted on a wooden sled. A horse pulled the line back into the woods after a log or turn of logs had been dragged to the landing. The animal was known as a "line horse" and had caulked shoes, just like his human counterparts. This was the first "ground lead" system of logging.

Power yarding at Gilley's logging camp in Burnaby. It was always a curiosity to see some men in old photos such as this dressed up in white shirts and vests. Were they posing for the camera or were they Bulls of the Woods who had no fear of getting dirty?

The first power yarding of logs carried out in the Pacific Northwest around 1890, according to L.B. Dixon ("Birth of the Lumber Industry in British Columbia"). As shown here, this spool affair utilized a vertical engine attached to an upright boiler. A "line horse" pulled the line back into the woods after the turn of logs had been dragged to the landing.

The next development was the replacement of the upright spool by a horizontal spool or drum for the "main line" and, as with the case of the first type, the horse was used to pull the line and "chokers", cables which were fastened around the log, hence, "choking" it, after each turn had been pulled out. An extra drum for the "haul back line" was the next innovation. This eliminated the horse from the woods in most instances because now the donkey could pull the main line back and forth.

Spar tree for high lead logging at Channel Logging Company, Vancouver Island, 1920.

The first steam donkey used in British Columbia was believed to be that owned by McIntyre Brothers at the Moodyville Company in 1897. There was a forerunner to this, a clumsy, wood and time-consuming steam tractor used for a time in 1875 at English Bay, now part of Vancouver's West End.

The early donkeys were crude and used the same sort of skid roads as the horses. Set on wooden sleds at the bottom of the road, they were, however, trendsetters for yarding timber from formerly inaccessible areas.

55

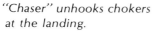
"Chaser" unhooks chokers at the landing.

Steel spar skidder at Franklin River on Vancouver Island. Logs were yarded in to portable steel "tree" and loaded onto railway flatcars.

McLean boom waiting for logs. Steampot donkey in background. Note rails where locie will pass with car for loading.

The "Walking Dudley" was a definite improvement over the immobile steam donkey in that it was a combination donkey and locomotive. It was bolted on a flatcar and ran on rails like a train engine, hauling itself up and down steep hills on cables on a drum. The first was used on Hollyburn Ridge, West Vancouver.

Just as machinery changed in the woods, so did the personnel required to operate a logging show. The basic crew at this juncture consisted of the Hooktender, Chokerman, Rigging Slinger and Whistle Punk.

The hooktender or "hooker" was undisputed boss of a yarding "side" or unit. The chokerman placed the chokers on the logs. Second in command to the hooker was the rigging slinger, "strawboss" of the chokerman. He picked out the log or logs to be taken. Lowest man on the totem pole, although he sat on a stump and not a pole, was the whistle punk. His job was to relay to the engineer the frequent signals that the rigging slinger shouted at him. The remaining members of the crew were the engineer who operated the donkey engine, a fireman to keep it fired up, woodcutters to cut its supply of fuel, and a Chaser, the man who unhooked the chokers at the log dump.

In the 1930s, the use of the gasoline engine started a trend to eliminate steam as generating power. Yarders using steam power were extremely difficult to move with their high boilers and their excessive water requirements which were a problem on dry hillsides. A great deal of backbreaking work was necessary to install pumps and great lengths of pipe. The use of the gas engine also reduced the hazard of fire. Then came the development of efficient diesel engines which took over from gasoline. Today, most logging equipment is diesel powered.

Shovel used in bridge building at Franklin River.

Miller Lumber Carrier operated by Mohawk Lumber Co. Ltd. in New Westminster, 1925.

Woodburning shovel used at Industrial Timber Mills, Camp 6, on Lake Cowichan in 1935.

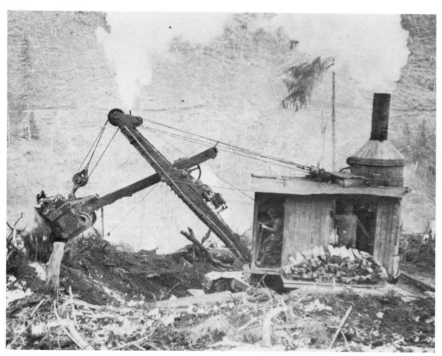

After trees are felled, they are delimbed and "bucked" (sawed into lengths) and dragged as much as 200 or 300 yards by a portable steel spar—such as this one—to the loading area. The operation is called "yarding". This mobile spar was used by Rayonier at Port McNeil.

Steel spars have replaced trees and carriers for steel spars are powered by the yarder engine rather than by a separate power unit as was the case with the initial steel spars.

Cranes, both tracked and rubber-tired, equipped with grapples or snorkels or both, have taken a lot of the labor out of loading.

Skidder and arch for yarding logs around 1947 and 1948.

Developments in the electronics industry will make logging even easier with closed circuit television and radio utilized over long distances. Balloon and helicopter logging are being seriously studied and in some areas put to actual use.

High-flying logger is the Okanagan Helicopters' pilot who is bringing in this turn of logs at Macmillan Bloedel's Cameron Lake Division northeast of Port Alberni. Experiments with helicopters and balloons are being taken seriously in the logging industry.

Unmentioned so far as an efficient and versatile machine which helped modernize and change logging is the tractor or "cat" (from the trade name Caterpillar). This tracked vehicle, or bulldozer, came into use in the woods of British Columbia in the Thirties when it was used mainly to clear roads but later, with the addition of an "arch", to yard logs.

Early Caterpillar hauling out a load of peeled power or telephone poles at Chase, B.C. Driver was right out in the action in this machine.

Owen Hennigar, Resident Manager at Canadian Forest Products Limited (CANFOR's) Englewood Logging Division, who started his career with Goffin, McNiven & Sores, recalls how dangerous and difficult to handle the first "cats" were. No canopies protected the driver from weather or falling debris. Later models featured a patented "Taylor" arch-shaped guard at the back of the driver. They were sometimes more hindrance than protection because a falling limb could hit the arch, which acted like a knife, lopping it off and showering the driver.

Bulldozer at work in the Camp 6 area of Industrial Timber Mills Ltd. on Lake Cowichan. The 75 horsepower Caterpillar was popular for road-building in the Forties, not so popular with operators who were unprotected from falling trees or rain and snow.

Owen Hennigar pulls in a turn of logs behind an old "cat" used at Camp "A" in the Beaver Cover area. Note the "arch" behind him, the driver's only protection against falling debris.

"They started to put proper guards over the driver around 1942," Hennigar said. Meantime, some men wore miner's hats made of bakelite but that material was too brittle to afford much protection and wouldn't stand up to the abuse taken by today's plastic protective headgear.

Aside from having tree limbs fall on him during his regular day's work, the worst that happened to Hennigar was when a cat he was driving slipped its brake while descending a steep grade with a load of logs in tow. This tractor was a difficult machine to handle and not at all like the fingertip controlled tractors of today. It had been well worn by the time Beaver Cove Timber Co. inherited it from Arrow Timber, where it had been used to take out Sitka spruce used in airplane manufacturing.

"Cat and arch" logging for Comox Logging and Railway Company at Ladysmith about 1937.

D-8 Caterpillar and mechanics at Camp "A", now Canadian Forest Products in Nimpkish Valley.

"I was foreman of the operation and one of the operators complained about the clutch and wanted me to check it out," Hennigar said. "It was all oiled up and slipping, but he failed to mention that the master cylinder on the brakes was shot too."

Everything went at once, including the machine, lickity split down the slope. Hennigar rode it down until it hit a stump and stopped. He was unhurt, unlike many unluckier men who were killed when their tractors rolled on them or a tree whipped back and smashed them against the arch.

A man named George Brooks, a gyppo (independent logger) in Bute Inlet in the Fifties, worked a small claim with his wife Verna and a seven-year-old son who could swear like a real logger. It was a "cat and arch" operation and it was a good life. George and Verna used the cat to drag logs from five or six big fir trees to the water's edge, buck them up in the water and form a boom. They would sell the logs and go to Vancouver where they lived in the best hotels until their money ran out, then they would go back to Bute Inlet and start all over again.

One working day, Brooks was steering the cat up a steep grade about 3,000 feet up a mountainside when he lost control of it and it began to slide backwards. Brooks dropped the 'dozer's blade to slow it down and wrapped his arms around the kid who, as always, was in the cab with him. The tractor slid over a bank and cut a swath through rocks, trees and stumps all the way down to the beach. It never turned around, slid sideways or altered course. George Brooks and his boy were safe and the machine sustained only a small amount of damage. It was clearly a miracle and the kid looked up at the mountain and then at Brooks: "Jeeezus, Dad!" he said. A true logger, thanking the Almighty.

Tractor in trouble. Bogged down in upper Nimpkish River.

Although not as important as formerly for dragging out logs, the bulldozer today is popular for road building and in helping control fire. This one is at work at Port McNeill for Rayonier.

The bulldozer tractor is still widely used for clearing and earthmoving jobs in the woods but its log hauling jobs are mostly done now by such as the giant-wheeled Timber Toter. The cat and the Timber Toter, in fact, might be considered the mechanical descendents of the horse and bull teams of the 1800s. But an element of excitement has gone right out of the scene with live animals' departure.

There's not much fun swearing at a machine.

61

Trees were regarded as "a beautiful accessory to the scenery" but had no commercial value or asset. The forest rape went on for many years.

5.
Cut And Get Out
The rape of the forests comes to an end.

"An epoch, sir, is drawing to a close—the epoch of reckless devastation of the natural resources with which we, the people of this fair young Province, have been endowed by Providence."

So spoke W.R. Ross, Minister of Lands in the Provincial Government of 1910. Ross was speaking in support of the Forest Act, enacted two years later, and condemning the epoch of "Cut And Get Out."

It was an era in which the forests were regarded merely as huge natural phenomena, endless and as unperishable as mountains, glaciers and rivers. They were a beautiful accessory to the scenery—to some—but regarded as having no value or commercial asset by many. Pioneers interested in farming the land found the trees a nuisance. An early edition of the New Westminster *Royal Columbian* tried to persuade city dwellers to regard them as a commercial crop: firewood. Wood was commanding up to four dollars and fifty cents a cord delivered to the steamers then plying the Fraser River. "A man would not only remove the timber so much dreaded from his lot but get (money) for his trouble," the newspaper said.

Since the timber was generally considered a nuisance, sale of forested land was encouraged by the government. By 1887, however, the prospective purchaser had to declare that the land he was taking up (pre-

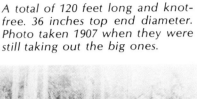

This majestic cedar was once standing near Ocean Falls. Picture taken about 1910.

A total of 120 feet long and knot-free. 36 inches top end diameter. Photo taken 1907 when they were still taking out the big ones.

Topping the spar tree at Franklin River on Vancouver Island.

empting) was for homesteading, and that the land would not be denuded of timber, then left. The Crown did reserve a royalty of twenty-five cents a thousand board feet, but land purchasers were not always conscientious in their declaration of timber values. In 1909 the Royal Commission of Inquiry on Timber and Forestry (also known as the Fulton Commission) recommended that Forest Rangers inspect properties which had been acquired ostensibly for settlement. By 1896 the sale of timberlands was prohibited and such lands were defined as having specified quantities: eight thousand board feet to the acre on the coast; five thousand feet in the Interior. In 1912 the British Columbia Forest Service was also formed and inspection proceedings were introduced. By that time the rape of some of the province's forests was well underway.

American logging companies, having butchered their own Eastern forests, looked greedily towards British Columbia. Because it lay closest to the lucrative Prairie market, the first area of the Province to receive attention was the East Kootenay region. The Prairie trade grew because immigration to this huge, largely treeless land was increasing at enormous speed. Farms, villages, and cities were blossoming everywhere and with the advent of the railroad, the demand for lumber was great.

Many pioneers regarded the trees on their land as a nuisance and something to be gotten rid of by any means possible. This is a typical Vancouver area scene of the late 1800s and even well into the 1900s.

Record one-horse load of 81 tons taken out of Weatherhead's camp at Yahk, B.C. (location: between Creston and Cranbrook). Date: around 1925.

This is one large tree that man didn't get the chance to cut down. It fell itself in December, 1886, and blocked the corner of Granville and Georgia Streets. Cut up and displayed from Toronto to London, England.

Another huge log, this one already peeled but not bucked up yet, at Gilley's camp in Burnaby. It was 72 feet 50 inches long.

Members of Vancouver and Nanaimo Boards of Trade visiting B. and T. Logging Company, Mt. Benson area, Nanaimo, 1934. The logs in this pic have been yarded from almost directly behind this group. Tidewater 12 miles, elevation 2,000 feet.

The comparatively untouched virgin stands of British Columbia were available for the taking and Americans rushed to make their claims, cruising almost every good available area between the years 1905 and 1910. A further stimulus to their investments was the widespread expectation that stumpage (assessment of worth) values would advance at least two dollars per 1,000 feet upon completion of the Panama Canal. In 1900 investment in British Columbia forest land was all-Canadian and amounted to about $2 million. By 1910 speculators and industrialists from United States owned ninety per cent of all investments in British Columbia forest. Total investment was $65 million.

A man could go anywhere on unoccupied Crown lands, put in a corner post, compose a rough description of one square mile of forest measured from that post, and thus secure from the Government exclusive right to the timber on that square mile, subject to the payment of a rent of $140 a year. (A stated condition was "no Chinese or Japanese to be employed in working the timber".) Such a square mile of forest was known as a "timber claim."

Frank Waters of the Council of Forest Industries, a non-profit association looking after various interests of a large number of forest companies, said at one time there were at least 4,000 handloggers on the British Columbia coast.

"They would just sail up in a skiff with all their equipment aboard, set up a tent camp, and start cutting logs." Waters said not all the handloggers made large fortunes because often they were not paid for their logs either by the brokers down south in Vancouver or by the sawmill. He also doubts that these "cut and get out" operators did very much to deplete the forests.

Handlogger at work in Teakerne Arm near Powell River. He is using the famous Gilchrist jack, along with which his crosscut saw, axes, sledge hammer, wedges and oil can made up his machinery. About 4,000 handloggers once worked along the coast and on coasts of Vancouver Island.

67

Two million lodge pole pine ties at
Hawkins Creek, 1928.

A typical handloggers' camp on the
B.C. coast. This one was established in 1940 but others back from
the turn of the century were dotted
throughout the inlets from Powell
River to Prince Rupert.

A truly huge load of logs for two horses to pull on a sleigh is this load cut by Columbia River Lumber Company on Horse Thief Creek, 1908-1909.

Another historian, Cecil Clark of Victoria, noted that larger operators did make money, "lots of it", often leaving their equipment to rust in the bush, considering it expendable.

M. Allerdale Grainger, Chief Forester-turned-author, described the influx of money-hungry timber cruisers in his book *Woodsmen of the West.* "They had staked the good timber, and then the poor timber, and then places that looked as if they had timber on them, and then places that lacked that appearance." Grainger reported that claims often were not staked to be logged but "sold to vague interests in United States" through advertisements placed in newspapers there.

Not surprisingly, the early lumbermen and timber speculators sought out the best timber, so many of the early licences and leases contained and still contain much of the finest timber in the Province. Established in the most accessible locations, they were mostly near tidewater along the southern coast and on Vancouver Island, often strategically positioned in the mouths of rivers or in valley bottoms.

More than seventy per cent of the total acreage now outstanding in old "temporary tenures" lies within the Vancouver Forest District. A Task Force report on Crown Charges For Early Timber Rights issued by the British Columbia Forest Service in 1974 states that through transactions in harvesting rights, mergers and the acquisition of one company by another, these tenures have become increasingly concentrated in the hands of a few corporations. It was noted that today nearly eighty per cent of the total acreage in these old "temporary tenures" is held by five timber firms and two non-operating trust companies; the latter have been assigned their holdings by two of the five timber firms for taxation purposes. In 1973, nearly seven decades since most of these rights were alienated, the old "temporary tenures" produced about 3.9 million cunits (each cunit containing 100 cubic feet), which accounted for 15.6 per cent of the total volume harvested from both private and public lands in the Province and 28.3 per cent of that cut in the Vancouver Forest District. What the Task Force is pointing out at this late date is that the early companies, and their successors, made some pretty good deals way back when.

The Crown, however, retained a financial interest in the timber alienated by it from 1887, and by 1896 it was government policy to retain title to any timbered land. In 1947 the sale was prohibited not only of timbered land but of any land that would find its "best economic use under a forest crop." Because of these provisions, at the present time the Crown (meaning the public) retains title to about ninety-three per cent of the estimated 118 million acres of productive forest land in British Columbia. Incidentally, that seven per cent of alienated land comprises not only ordinary alienations such as those already mentioned, but also large grants made to encourage railway building. The largest of these is the Canadian Pacific-owned Esquimalt & Nanaimo Railway land grant, originally for nearly one-third of Vancouver Island, consisting of 3,000 square miles of the finest forest land in the Province! This land, granted by the Province to the Dominion Government, was in turn granted to a private company which became a subsidiary of the Canadian Pacific Railway. For years the Canadian Pacific Railway made a practice of selling the land and the timber but around 1961 started to manage what is still held on a sustained yield basis. The company now owns or controls several logging firms on Vancouver Island.

One of the reasons the Crown retains as much land as it does is because, before and after 1907, many of the tenures reverted following the removal of the virgin timber—as was intended. But many more reverted by default with the timber intact when the prospects for the forest industry appeared less auspicious or when licences recklessly staked out were found to be less valuable than supposed. These are legacies British Columbians have inherited from the lack of foresight of earlier governments when economic conditions were vastly different from those today. There is no intention to condemn the individuals who profited from the situation, but, like Lands Minister Ross, to condemn the "epoch" that provided such advantage.

An example of the rate of growth in the lumbering industry during this boom period is that of Elk Lumber and Manufacturing Company which sprang up at Fernie.

In the peak year of 1907 Elk Lumber cut 25 million board feet of lumber. To continue cutting at such a rate would have been impossible. Towns were built and prospered but as the stands of timber were depleted or became inaccessible because of distance or difficulties of terrain, they closed down. The list of once prosperous communities established between 1900 and 1910 which depended for their existence upon the forest resources only to become ghost towns, is formidable. A typical story is that of the Adolph Lumber Company located at Baynes Lake. This mill cut 75 thousand feet of lumber a day. By 1923 there was no lumber accessible to the mill so it was forced to close. In the town of Waldo, between Fernie and the Montana border, Baker Lumber Company and Saskatoon Company competed with each other for the larger cut. The forest resources were depleted by 1929. Waldo did not disappear, like so many of the early communities, but is a small farming community today.

A town that did virtually return to the soil is the community of Lumberton, once the site of the largest sawmill in the interior of the Province.

Skidder with separate loading machine. See rail cars on which logs are being loaded. Probably Industrial Timber Company at Cowichan Lake.

Cranbrook Forest Products at Bull River took out this load of yellow pine logs by horse and wagon in 1912.

These oldtime fallers spent most of the day cutting down this magnificent fir.

71

"Michigan Big Wheels" at Canyon, B.C. around 1910.

Horse drawn logging wheels, sometimes called "Michigan Big Wheels", driven by teamsters for Crow's Nest Pass Lumber Company which had operations in Wardner, Galloway, Elko area near Fernie. Photo taken 1921.

The operation represented an investment of only $2 million by British Columbia Spruce Mills Ltd.—a Wisconsin firm. During the peak period a daily cut of some 150 thousand feet was standard. A population of 250 people lived in Lumberton, which boasted modern housing, store, recreation hall, post office and garage. Many mill workers there came from Cranbrook and the payroll of about $50,000 a month was mostly spent in that developing city. However, in the late Thirties most of the accessible timber had been cut and what the rapacious mill hadn't devoured, forest fires had. In some years the destruction by fire was greater than that caused by logging.

Logging interests and the government itself, prior to this time and for some years later, were under the impression that natural reforestation would take place. They had only to look to the example of the American Midwest to see the result of nature recovering. This does not happen overnight.

A step in the direction towards rectifying the bad years came in 1912 at the same time the Forest Act was introduced. The Forest Protection Fund was set up with timber owners contributing twelve cents an acre and the government matching the investment dollar for dollar. The Commission members who suggested the legislation leading to the Forest Act said in their report that they had been assured logging operations in the Province were "in the hands of practical businessmen engaged in supplying a certain market demand for lumber and that the forest was receiving the best treatment that was commercially possible." However, the Commissioners had observed forest exploitation results in other countries and discovered that in the early developments of lumbering, cheap stumpage was seen to have been accompanied by butchery of wood. Loggers everywhere were leaving tree tops up to ten inches and six and eight-foot high stumps to rot behind them. "Human nature," the Commissioners said, "is careless of everything of low commercial value, especially when the supply seems inexhaustible and waste costs nothing to the waster." They noted that when stumpage rates rose, this state of affairs came to an end. Operators were asked to pay for the merchantable timber operated on, not merely for the portion their workmen chose to cull.

Horses used near Campbell River to drag out huge logs like these which will be pulled forward to the logs shown in the foreground, then rolled into position for transporting by boom to mill.

73

Thirty years later a Royal Commission headed by Chief Justice Gordon Sloan was set up and in December, 1945, its report was handed down, its main result being the inauguration of a Sustained Yield Policy. Legislation was presented bringing into effect what were first known as Forest Management Licences, now known as Tree Farm Licences. A Tree Farm Licence is a combination of Crown grant timber, of licences and leases, and of previously unalienated Crown timber. Its term was originally in perpetuity but in 1957 the Act was amended to provide for a twenty-one year renewable term. Tree Farm Licences became somewhat politically undesirable when one cabinet minister in a former government was convicted of taking bribes. For this and other reasons the Crown began in the mid-1950s to set up what are now known as Public Sustained Yield Units. These are areas of Crown land usually in excess of one million acres and defined by topographic features such as rivers and mountains. There are currently seventy-eight such units covering over 80 million acres and more are planned for northern regions.

In 1955 Chief Justice Sloan was again appointed sole Commissioner of a Royal Commission to inquire into the status of the forest resource. In his report presented in July, 1957, he recommended—among other things—that no further Tree Farm Licences be granted in the Interior of British Columbia except in remote, undeveloped areas and then only for full utilization. He further recommended that only minor areas should be removed from the Public Sustained Yield Units for Tree Farm licence purposes.

The Forest Act of 1912, the earlier Fulton Report, the two Sloan Commissions, all have acted to stabilize the lumbering industry and to make it yield close to its full potential, not only for the big companies but for the small independents, as well as for the citizens of British Columbia.

More changes are in the wind. The Task Force on Crown Timber Disposal has recommended that the present schedule of royalties applied to the old "temporary" tenures, set out in the Forest Act, be abolished in favor of royalty assessments. These would be based on forest appraisals such as those already applied to other Crown timber. This would mean the holders of these tenures—the few large corporations controlling timber rights in those easily accessible areas in Vancouver Forest District—will have to pay more for them.

Log flume of the Crow's Nest Pass Lumber Company near Bull River in the Fernie area, 1910-1914.

This magnificent display of Douglas fir stands as a reminder of what trees in British Columbia used to be like. They're in Cathedral Grove on the Port Alberni Road on Vancouver Island.

Ready to make undercut are these two early loggers at Myrtle Point camp of Bloedel, Stewart and Welch in 1926.

6.
From Bullcook to Bull of the Woods

The "characters"

The "characters", like Seven Day Wilson, Step And A Half Phelps, Panicky Bell, Porkchop Larsen, Two Dollar Smith, Rough House Pete, the Sockless Swede and Gasoline Mike made British Columbia's forests a lively place to work.

Throughout logging history there have been colorful men and women who helped make the woods of British Columbia an interesting place to live and work. Many of these individuals have since gone to cut lumber in the Big Timber Mill in the Sky, but others are still around, still creating legends.

One is Jack Bell, recently retired as general foreman at the Northwest Bay Division of MacMillan Bloedel, who once fell ninety feet out of a spar tree, got his broken leg mended, and went right back highrigging. Bell knew many of the oldtime logging characters including Seattle Red, Step And A Half Phelps, Seven Day Wilson, and others.

Probably the best known of the oldtimers is Seven Day Wilson, who had one claim to fame: but for one occasion, he never worked a day over a week at any one camp, although somehow he managed to spend most of his life in the logging industry. Wilson once outsmarted himself while working at Matt Hemmingsen's camp at the head of Lake Cowichan, however. He had worked the seventh and holy day and it was time he rested. In the bunkhouse, as he yanked off his caulk boots, he bragged of the tradition that required that he pull stakes. The other loggers razzed him about his short work span and Wilson rankled. "I'll tell you what I'll do," He said. "I'll throw this boot here up in the air and if it stays up I'll stay another seven days." With a confident grin, he threw the boot. Unfortunately for Wilson's reputation, the boot stayed up. It wound up in a chimney hole. He was bound to stay on and observers say his next trip to town was twice as long and twice as good.

Jack Bell says Seattle Red spent even less time at each camp than Seven Day Wilson. Seattle Red wandered from camp to camp, from British Columbia to California . . . wandered, not worked. Hired late in the afternoon, Seattle Red would wash up, eat with the crew coming in that afternoon, sleep in the bunkhouse that night, wash up in the morning, eat a hearty breakfast, and then, just as everyone else was heading for a hard day's work in the woods, quit.

Veteran logger Jack Bell retired as general manager at MacMillan Bloedel's Northwest Bay Division in 1975. This photo of him rigging a Ledgerwood steel spar was taken in 1938. Bell spent 10 years as a highrigger at MB Franklin River operation and suffered only one accident. He fell 90 feet from a spar tree and only broke a leg.

Fraser Creek camp of British Columbia Forest Products Limited during 1950s.

Another favorite character Bell yarned about is Porkchop Larsen, one of the meanest cooks ever to wield a meatcleaver. Long Pete, another burly cook with a wafer-thin temper, pounded many a diner into the cookhouse floor for the cardinal sin of complaining about the cuisine. Such logging camp cooks are a favorite topic of conversation for loggers. Some recall a cook at Taylor Brothers' camp on Bute Inlet. The fact that she had only one arm impaired neither her cooking skill nor her courage. One night she heard a noise near her meat shack and hustled out, temper blazing, her good arm hooked around a broom. A logger shone a light into the pitch black and shouted at her: "Jenny. Get away from there. That's a grizzly bear you're hitting with that broomstick." "I don't care what it is," Jenny yelled back. "Nobody's gonna get *my* meat!"

A little action taking place down at the donkey. Bernard Timber & Logging Co. at Orford Bay in Bute Inlet, 1926. From the Roozeboom Collection of fine photographs at Provincial Archives.

79

Woss Camp cookshack. It didn't pay to cross the cook or the bullcook. It also paid to wait until you got some seniority before you got lippy over grub.

When the going gets rough, ask a horse for help. This old steam engine needed team to get started in Hoff Lumber camp near Fort St. James. Claude Richter at reins.

As well as favorite cook stories, loggers have favorite cooks. Some rated George Jenks the best cook on the coast; in the Interior they'll tell you about "King" Cole, Bob Daily, and Scotty Middlemas, head cook at the Fort Garry Tie Camp in 1926. His baking powder biscuits would melt in your mouth, it's said. Here is the recipe as it appeared in an old scrapbook. (Use at your own discretion!)

> 1 cup lard
> 4 cups flour
> 2 heaping teaspoons baking powder
> 1 level teaspoon salt

Mix with water. Don't handle too much. Cut and paint with canned milk. Cook in fast oven. Never look before fifteen minutes. Eat.

Another favorite subject—whenever loggers get together to swap lies—is talking about the best or worst bullcook they have ever known. Bullcooks, as you will know by now, make beds, sweep out bunkhouses and generally make themselves useful around camp. Many of them have been loggers all their lives until liquor and circumstances have united to bring about their downfall, so they finish their lives right where it all began for them. Ex-logger George Haywood tells of the old "alkie" bullcook at Bloedel's Great Central Lake camp who loved shaving lotion. He drank everybody's, but not all at once. "He had style," Haywood said. "You'd go to shave and notice that your lotion was going down faster than your beard, then one day it'd be gone completely, and so would the bullcook—into town on a toot." But he was an honest thief. "When he came back, the first thing he did was replace your bottle of shaving lotion with a new full one," Haywood said. "Then in a couple of weeks, when he'd run out of everything else to drink, you'd find your lotion going down again."

Cold deck pile at Chief Lake, 1944. C.B. Hoff Sawmill. Timbers were cut into 2 by 10's, 20-feet long. Dunning Hoff with horse.

Stories about the Loganberry Lancers, one of the more polite names given to men who drink anything including extracts, are legion among loggers. One concerns Zeke, a superintendent on a Garibaldi Mountain haywire show. One day Zeke bawled out his crew for leaving alcohol around for the cook to get drunk on. Then, one day, he and some of his men found the cook, half-drowned in lemon extract, on the cookshack floor. "I sure hope the cook doesn't find out about that big alcohol compass on the boat," a logger remarked at the time. "That sure was a dumb thing to say," another logger told him after the incident. "Zeke is worse than the cook. He'll drink anything." Sure enough, next day when they checked the boat, the compass was dry as the desert.

In another story involving Zeke, he was standing on a stump one day directing things from the spar tree, so bleary and hungover he couldn't see he was in the bight of the haulback, a dangerous spot to say the least. A sapling holding the line snapped and like a bowstring tightening, shot Zeke like an arrow for about seventy feet. He came down next to another Abbott Street refugee who was pulling rigging at that point. Zeke was bleeding and yelling in pain.

"Aw shaddup!" the other man said. "That's only the shoe polish comin' out so far!"

Just for the record, Zeke survived his trip and eventually returned to the same camp, not as superintendent this time, but as bullcook.

The only ones who smiled for the camera were the horses. A logging scene in B.C. probably in the Twenties or earlier, location also unknown.

82

Magnificent Fake . . . Controversy still rages around this photograph which is generally considered by authorities to be faked. Human figures were superimposed on what was supposed to be a 417-foot high, 25-foot diameter fir. Vancouver lumberman fooled their rival American loggers that B.C. really did have the biggest trees.

Another bullcook with a reputation as a heavy drinker was Old Swede Charlie of Sooke. He came back to Elder's camp after a particularly heavy evening in Victoria and headed for the outdoor privy which had only a pole across to separate man from manhole.

After an hour or two someone else felt nature's urge and came back to report that Old Swede had fallen on bad times. A work party was dispatched to get the old man out but he never lived down the experience.

Hungry Bill, a logger at Youbou in the Lake Cowichan country, had read in the newspaper that life-saving penicillin was made from the mold on stale bread. So Bill used to cadge all the bread he could from the cookshack and keep it in the bunkhouse under his bed until even loggers with the most insensitive noses began to wonder where the smell was coming from. Bill would decide by then that the bread was green enough to eat. No one knew what it was that Hungry Bill was suffering from, but he must have figured that if mold was good enough for whatever penicillin killed, it was good enough for him and his.

Taking a break before even beginning what will be a mammoth task are these two loggers working for Brooks, Scanlon and O'Brian at Stillwater, 1926.

Panicky Bell, general superintendent at Silver Skagit Lumber, was approached one day by a furious logger who showed him some rancid meat in his sandwich. "It's green," the logger said. "What color would you *like?*" Bell asked.

Big Bill Moraski was a 240-pound highrigger built like a bull, with a voice to match, but he moved like a cat up a tree. His specialty was to trim the spar tree, top it, then stand on top and spread his arms like a thunderbird on a totem pole. Another logger, equally strong, who also

83

A spare highrigger at Woss Camp. Bud Frost, first cougar hunter to be engaged by a logging firm, took the picture. Bruin worked for good wages of berries and occasional bees' nests.

performed an act of derring-do on the tree top, once packed out a freshly killed deer on his back. Big Bill Burgess had worked as a sparring partner for Jack Dempsey and was no man to mess around with when it came to a fight.

Two Dollar Smith was a man-catcher, one of the company representatives who went searching through hotel beer parlors for loggers who might be ready to take on another spell in the woods. Most men the man-catcher caught were broke and ready for a "drag" to get back. Some outfits would spring for as much as fifty dollars so a logger could redeem his boots from the pawnbroker and perhaps buy some liquor to see him through the rough moments on the trip back. Two Dollar Smith did not offer fifty dollars. Two Dollar Smith offered two dollars. He is remembered.

Handloggers making undercut on big fir. Working alone or in pairs the hand-logger's life was quiet but had own rewards, as long as they stayed healthy and didn't get hurt. They might die without available medical attention.

An example of the reputation for excessive drinking some loggers have gained through the years is recounted in the story sent down through time by British Columbia writer Francis Dickie. It happened about fifty years ago when some handloggers dropped into a wilderness hotel of the type that flourished wherever there were men and dry throats. Six worthies were stakey and after several months spent falling and moving logs to the water's edge, they had decided to spend a solid week slaking their throats at this particular little hotel. When Saturday night finally passed into oblivion along with the six handloggers, the exhausted hotelier knew he'd had enough of tending bar and decided to close it until Monday morning. Sunday morning came and the handloggers rose, parched and surly, and set up a chorus outside the hotelman's bedroom. " Open up the bar or we'll dump your hotel into the sea." The proprietor was as stubborn as he was tired and he refused in language as befitted the forest and the time. After a few more entreaties, the hangover voices retreated and within moments the small building began to rise on one side. It was the side away from the sheer rock cliff that rose up from the salt chuck. The handloggers had fetched their Gilchrist jacks and were lifting up the hotel. The hotelman knew when he was licked and quickly unbolted the barroom door. The loggers abandoned their jacks with alacrity to quench their thirst in a manner suitable to their victory.

Horses pulling railway flatcar with load of logs along railway track at Hazelmere, south of Cloverdale, 1912. McKay and Flannigan Logging crew.

Handlogger making undercut on log. This is only way to keep log from jamming saw, by cutting beneath and above. Notice crosscut is being held in position by double-bitted axe.

85

Waterwheel constructed by timber cruisers and foresters for B.C. Forest Products near Bear Creek Camp, southern Vancouver Island, 1949.

This story has a parallel in modern times: a gyppo logger was hoisting a noisy few at a hotel on a northeast coast island famous for its beer sales. At one point the gyppo became objectionable, that is to say, obnoxious, questioning even the parenthood of the waiter and bartender who assisted him to the door. His exit was ungracious, even by logger standards, and he vowed on his honor to return and stern would be the consequences. The waiter and bartender didn't care. In their opinion they had thrown better patrons *into* the beer parlor. They forgot the incident. Four days later the gyppo strolled into the beer parlor with a smile that was a pure mixture of Mona Lisa and Cheshire Cat. The waiter, a forgiving sort, inquired if he would consent to a cool beer at the going price and the gyppo replied that indeed he would. "And have one for yourself," he said, with ominous charity. "It'll be the last one you'll be having in this hotel."

"What do you mean?" the waiter said, dander rising. "You're fired," the gyppo said. "You and all the rest of you here. You can pack your duds and hit for the next boat." It seems that our hero had gone to Vancouver, contacted the owner of the hotel, made him an offer he couldn't refuse, and became owner of the inn. Who says Diamond Jim Brady is dead?

86

"This is the view of the world I get all day?" Logger takes dim view but keeps plugging along.

Hughie Cliffe of Ladysmith, who began his long career greasing skids on what was Vancouver's original skid road, knew some of the big names in logging at the turn of the century and could reel them off the way some people can recite the names of hockey greats! There was Big John Mackenzie who ran the Hastings Mill; Abe MacLaughlin who had a logging show at Fanny Bay on Vancouver Island, and Don Anthony who worked stands on Thurlow Island. Also Step And A Half Phelps, a man to be reckoned with. Phelps was a real highballer who brooked no nonsense from anyone. Superintendent at Pioneer Timber at Port McNeill, he ran a tight camp. His motto was "Up the Hill or Down the Channel", and when he fired a man he always asked if he had any friends in camp. They were fired too. He got his name because of his peculiar gait, but loggers talked about him only behind his back. He had no respect for Sunday loggers or dandies who overdressed for the job. A rope belt was a badge of courage. "Send me up a couple of chokermen," Phelps would say. "If they wear caps and belts, send me four." If he didn't like the look of your undercut he'd ask: "Do you play play bridge? I'll get you three more so you won't be lonesome going back!"

But just about the toughest bush ape ever to strap on leg irons and walk upright was Pete Ohlson, the "Rough House Pete" immortalized in Robert E. Swanson's poem.

In the days of bull-team logging, when they hauled logs on
    the skid,
And they cut the stumps way above the swell;
It was then I hit the jungle—I was only just a kid,
But the roughest, toughest kid this side of hell.
I could lick a cougar cat, if a man should drop a hat,
And I'd kicked my way from jail with flying feet:
California to Alaska—I was famous just for that,
And so far and wide they hailed me, "Rough House Pete."

Columbia River Lumber Company freight teams with lumber, hay and other supplies, around 1907, 1908.

The pause that refreshes. British Columbia Forest Products Limited forester at Cabin Creek campsite, 1949. It's not hard to see our friend had an ocean voyage, judging by the origin of that towel.

88

Coffee break on the "Kla-anch Mainline (Nimpkish) Railroad" in 1954. Left to right in this sitdown construction crew are: Ole Blansheim, powderpacker; Ole Holter, powderman; Charlie Clark, powderman; Sid Stewart, cat driver; Albert Damery, swamper; M. Cooper, shovel operator.

D.L. McMullan, surveyor, at Lake Cowichan Camp 6 area, 1935, while working for Industrial Timber Mills.

Ohlson was working as a hooktender for an outfit near Squamish when he decided to pull the pin, that is, quit. After supper he went to the time-keeper and demanded his pay. "You can't have your time until you've turned in your tools," the man said. So Pete rounded up his crew and a locomotive which he hooked onto the donkey engine. The big ma-chine came down, dragging a snarl of shackles, lines and blocks, to the office steps. "Okay," Ohlson said to the timekeeper, jerking his thumb at the mess outside. "Here's my tools. Now give me my time."

Not all men of great size were brawlers. Big Alex Stewart logged the Cowichan Valley and Hornby Island in the Twenties. Big Alex was six foot six and weighed 260 pounds. But he was a gentleman, remembered for his gimpy leg, Durant car and pet pig. "Chin Whisker" Anderson was a logging operator who earned the undying respect and devotion of his men. Chin Whisker introduced into his bunkhouse an innovation that spoiled his men for all time and all other camps: the enamelled pot or "thundermug." The pots were a touch of luxury that appeared al-most out of keeping with the burly nature of the loggers of that day, men who were used to staggering out of the bunkhouse and into the woods when the call of nature came.

More in character were the operators who worked the logging shows in the rugged country near Ocean Falls: Dirty Dan McLusky, the Sock-less Swede and Gasoline Mike. There were others sprinkled around the Province: Black Mike, White Mike, and a cardsharp who only logged as a method of getting into high stakes poker games on the weekends: Seven Draw Pete.

89

There were nice women like Elsie Taylor, a Howe Sound cook so pretty that she never needed flunkys because the loggers lined up to help with dishes; then there were the others, the camp followers, the ladies who worked the loggers who worked the logs. Some gained permanent reputations in places like the "Goat Farm" near Port Alberni and at "Pecker Point" on the way to Ocean Falls. Others did their business from trailer houses set up at the fringes of the camps, then moving on to the next neck in the woods when the police got wind of them.

The men at sea established reputations as characters too. Charlie Goodwin, skipper of the Island Tug & Barge *Island Commander*, was a man to chew snoose. The *Commander*, a former North Sea trawler with a whaleback bow, had been built in Scotland in 1911. An outside ladder climbing past the wheelhouse window was the only way to get from the main deck to the boat deck. Cook Bill Loeppky recalls that Charlie used to spit out the wheelhouse window so the rail usually was covered with a goodly amount of the dark brown substance. "The worse the weather, the more the snoose," Loeppky said. "On a really bad night, with the wind howling and the sea boiling and Charlie spitting, it was rare indeed not to return from the boat deck without a handful of it."

Four teams of horses pulling four huge sleighloads of logs out of Aleza Lake sometime in the early 1900s.

Another man on the tugs who enjoyed the bad weather was Hurricane Harry Olney, a 300-pound captain from Alert Bay who got his kicks from riding out the big storms. The worse the weather the better Olney liked it. It came from being from a long line of fearless Indians who rode out in canoes and faced down storms that would break the spirit of the squeamish. Olney's motto was: "Wait till the wind hits forty, then we'll go. And if that doesn't work, we'll try something else."

There's another story about Hurricane Harry: He was breaking in a new mate while towing a boom of logs through Dodds Narrows near Nanaimo. The tide was fast, about eighteen knots, and the mate was nervous. The area, as usual in summertime, was dotted with pleasure craft. "What do I do if I meet a little boat in the Narrows?" the new mate asked. "Take your half," Hurricane Harry told him. "But make sure you take your half out in the *middle*."

Jack McNeil's cabin at Camp 5, Block 1, west of Ladysmith. Mrs. McNeil sitting in front. The cabin was built on a Sunday at a cost of 5 bottles of whiskey. Mrs. McNeil looks reasonably pleased.

"Good Grief! I gave up a good job in an office in Vancouver to work in the rain in the bush?" Suzanne McSorley can be forgiven for entertaining such doubts of judgment on a rainy day like this. She's a "lumberjill" for Rayonier.

91

The cliffs at Bute Inlet, with their melting snows and heavy spring run-off, have a tendency to slip away at times, as one logger found out. Left to caretake the camp while all the others went to town, he was in the privy at the Bear Bay operation, contemplating life. A sound that started as a rumble and grew to a roar brought him out of his reverie. The earth began to shake and he found himself observing a Caterpillar tractor and truck gliding in a flood of mud down the slope towards the salt chuck. Before he could alter his position or reach for the Eaton's catalogue, the bunkhouse, cookshack and woodpile slid past him. When the slide ended, the outhouse was the only visible evidence that a logging camp had ever stood on that sidehill. It was a moving experience!

Loading rail cars with logs at Crow's Nest Pass Lumber Company, 1921.

Brooks, Scanlon and O'Brian, Stillwater, B.C. around 1926.

A favorite story concerns Morgan Scott, now Mrs. Morgan Ostler of West Vancouver, who was visiting her sister Maureen, a school teacher at a logging camp in the Nimpkish Valley on Vancouver Island. Morgan was royally wined and danced off her feet by the young loggers there who had already made a queen of her sister by vying for the privilege of cutting wood for her teacherage—Maureen had the biggest woodpile in the valley. When the dancing was done, Morgan welcomed an invitation to flop onto a Winnipeg couch which had been set up for her use at the home of a married couple who lived in the camp.

It was a moonlit night and Morgan slept soundly until a rustling sound awakened her. She opened her eyes and discovered another pair of eyes staring back. These eyes were set in a huge face, fringed by red hair and beard. The face was only a foot from her own since the man who owned it was on his hands and knees. Or, to be more specific, on *hand* and knees, the one hand being under the bed. Morgan was too scared to scream and, besides, the man cautioned her not to do so by gestures. Then in tones sweet and low he said: "Sorry to bother you ma'am. I just come in here to get a jar of wine." That didn't do much to calm Morgan's racing pulse but the man's exit on all fours did. He was bearing a jug of red liquid judged by appearances to be wine. The next morning, before the visitor got a chance to tell her hostess about her nocturnal prowler, she happened to peer behind a curtain which covered one entire wall. It was a ceiling-to-floor shelf, covered with home brew wine. Her hostess was the local bootlegger.

Not all stories of logging country characters are about the rough and tough ones. These stories don't get told but it is typical of their generosity for loggers to donate money to good causes or otherwise do good

92

turns. One group of loggers bought a cow for the Victorian Order of Nurses when they and Reverend John Antle of the Columbia Coast Mission opened a cottage hospital at Rock Bay. When one of their favorite nurses died, the loggers made her a coffin and lined it with wild spirea as a token of their love and respect.

Bud Frost of Port Alberni gets into this chapter also, not because he is a "character" but because of the unique jobs he has held. Frost was the only professional cougar hunter ever hired by a logging company as its recreation officer. Canadian Forest Products at Englewood hired him to control the cougars that wandered into their Nimpkish River camps to snatch domestic cats and dogs in the backyards of employees' homes. A former logger who slung rigging for Bloedel at Great Central Lake and whistle-punked for Alberni Pacific when he was only sixteen, Frost moved into Woss Camp with one each of Blue Tick, Fox, and Black and Tan hounds. He built a dog kennel and went to work. If he came across cougar signs close to a camp while cruising and mapping, he would run for the dogs, tree the animal, and shoot it. Nevertheless, he retains an enormous respect for the big cats; cougars have a vital place in the Cosmic Order he says, remarking also that humans are out of step when they corner a cougar or keep a domestic pet in an area which is cougar country. Cougars help control animal population.

As time goes by, anecdotes about logging "characters" will continue to extend beyond the truth. Some say the times are too tame and organized for individuals to flourish anymore. Bets are down they're wrong.

Sasquatch or Mugwamp? Cougar hunter Bud Frost examines this curious stump formation in Nimpkish Valley.

93

First train to arrive in Vancouver, "a land not worth keeping." Note stack of lumber on wharf.

7.
Steam Rising
From Old Curly to Diesel.

"British Columbia is a barren, cold mountain country that is not worth keeping," the editor of the British magazine *Truth* wrote in 1881. "Fifty railroads would not galvanize it into prosperity." The editor was condemning attempts to raise money in Britain by promoters of the Canadian Pacific Railroad who wanted to tie Canada together with a steel ribbon. Despite the discouraging words of *Truth's* editor, railroad builder William Van Horne completed tying the ribbon in 1885.

"Old Curly" as she was originally. Bob Harvey, engineer, looking out of window. Percy DesBrisay in white shirt leaning against logs. Original photo taken in 1894 at Saul Reamy camp on Thurlow Island. Oxen or horses must also have been used. See watering trough and hay, also skidroad on right side of photo.

Other railroads that came steaming onto the scene after that time also helped galvanize British Columbia "into prosperity." These were the logging railroads and by 1917 there were not fifty, but sixty-two of them, with ninety-eight locomotives and 354 flatcars, utilizing 40 miles of track. A new era had opened up in the annals of logging transportation. Steaming giants and dwarves went deeper and deeper every year into coastal and Vancouver Island valleys where trestles of immense height were built to gulf impossible terrain.

View of 60 ton Climax geared locomotive trailing logs between the rails for the Victoria Lumber and Manufacturing Company, Vancouver Island.

Pole road using an 8-wheel, 15 ton upright Climax geared locomotive. Style "A". It was only serviceable on comparatively level tracks where the ground was soft and would not warrant the expense of a wooden stringer or steel rail track. A number of this type were in use in British Columbia. Notice bulls are positioned to pull up logs onto railcar with help of men with peaveys.

In early operations, however, the locomotives were used to skid logs in a manner similar to that employing animals, pulling logs between rails spiked to the skidroads. Log rails were often used instead of steel, but the land had to be level. The system was used with success in areas where the land was also either too soft or the timber too sparse to make laying proper ties and steel rails economical. When logging began to leave the flats and valley bottoms, geared locomotives such as the Pacific Coast Shay and Climax operated on the steeper spurs while larger rod locomotives like the "Baldwin" were used on the main lines. The Climax had a piston on each side which fired alternately, while the Shay had three side-mounted cylinders and geared driveshaft. Another locomotive was the Heisler, "the Cadillac of the logging locies", which was a combination between a geared locomotive and a conventional rod engine with both gears and side rods. The rod engines were also especially adapted for logging by the addition of saddle tanks which placed nearly all weight on "drivers" and incorporated very small wheels.

Shawnigan Lake Lumber Company locie show in 1902.

Shawnigan Lake Lumber Company in 1903.

There is still a lot of controversy about where the first steam locomotive was used for logging in British Columbia. A little locomotive called "Curly" now standing as a relic in Hastings Park in Vancouver is said to be the first to be used by a logging firm. A tablet on the exhibit records that this locie was used in the building of the Panama Canal then brought to British Columbia by the Canadian Pacific Railway to work on the railroad construction through the Rockies; eventually it was purchased from the railroad by Hastings Sawmill Company for its logging operations at Thurlow Inlet and Quadra Island. Camp foreman Saul Reamy used it there to haul logs in 1901 and later it was barged to Rock Bay, another logging site between Campbell River and Kelsey Bay.

Early day steam engine used in hauling logs. On display at British Columbia Forest Museum near Duncan on Vancouver Island.

Steam engine used for a shingle mill at Sullivan (West Surrey).

Rolling logs from railway cars into Shawnigan Lake, 1917.

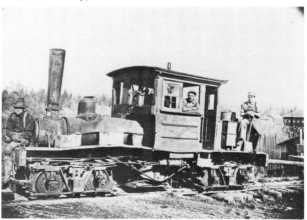

98

Railroad authority Robert E. Swanson of Vancouver declares that the first logging locomotive was operated at Chemainus in 1900 by an individual named Hickory Palmer. Swanson, former chief engineer of the provincial Department of Commercial Transport, says Palmer used a forty-five ton Climax to drag logs down a skidroad from Miller Creek. He says it was probably oldtime lumberman Matt Hemmingsen who first decided to spike railroad steel onto the skidroad and have a locie drag the logs between the rails. This type of skidding operation became obsolete by 1910; by then all logging railroads in the province had converted to steel rails on regular railroad ties.

During this time Victoria Lumber and Manufacturing Company at Chemainus imported a rod engine known as Number 21 from Pennsylvania and adapted flatcars to carry logs. Instead of the special logging cars as we know them today, these early log carriers were sets of old "trucks" from under railway boxcars upon which "bunks" had been attached to cradle the logs. Each of the four railcar wheels on these conveyances had its own brake which had to be set separately. This led to a great deal of action and many accidents, both of which were visited upon the unfortunate brakeman who had to leap from car to car and across piles of swaying logs which were held from rolling by "cheese blocks", wedges of wood or metal, jammed under them at intervals. Later on, the cars had wooden stakes at the corners which were broken off to release the logs at the dump. This was not the job of the "brakie", who was kept busy enough setting the brakes and coupling and uncoupling the cars. The engineer would indicate by a certain whistle how tight he wanted the brakes set and the brakie would oblige. It was dangerous work and until the advent of air brakes brakemen lost arms, legs and feet. Many were killed. By 1925 air brakes and standard couplers, which did not require human participation, were on all logging railroad cars.

Loading the flat car of the train at Kings, South Surrey, B.C., around 1917.

Early day loggers had their work cut out for them in this daily chore: cutting up the cordwood for the locomotives to use. Origin of photo is not known, but could have been any camp in Pacific Northwest.

99

Of the hundreds of railroad locomotives once used in logging in British Columbia, few remain. Those that do have storied careers. When the Hastings Company finished their operations at Rock Bay, another private company, Merrill, Ring & Wilson, moved in. They operated a large railroad show which included two ninety-ton Pacific Coast Shays and several Climaxes to haul logs thirty miles to the beach. When the company left Rock Bay in 1941 the Number 5 Shay went to Hillcrest Lumber Company at Mesachie Lake and Number 4 Shay went to Dewey Anderson's claim at Kelsey Bay. Number 4 then went to "Panicky" Bell's outfit on the Queen Charlotte Islands and Number 5 operated for Russell Mills, of bridge-building fame, at Englewood. In 1962, the Number 5 was put to switching on the wharves in North Vancouver and proved so successful that Mayo Lumber Company's big Number 4 Shay was brought from Nanaimo to work beside her sister machine. Both are still in existence: Number 4 was sold to the State of West Virginia and Number 5 was donated to Fort Steele Museum at Cranbrook where it now operates as a tourist attraction.

One of the original locomotives operated near Courtenay now performs services on a sometimes basis at a recreational railroad known as Victoria Pacific at Millstream Junction, just west of Victoria. Number 7, a little saddle tank engine that used to be Number 2 of the Pacific Great Eastern (now British Columbia Railway) is now a monument at Squamish, British Columbia. Crown Zellerbach's logging equipment and arboretum exhibit in Ladysmith features two old locies; under a sequoia stands Number 12, a fifty-ton Shay that hauled logs all over British Columbia. Number 11, in the shade of a Cedar of Lebanon, is a Baldwin rod engine built in 1923.

A real story of durability lies behind the forty-five ton wood-burning Shay now on display at the entrance to British Columbia Forest Museum five miles north of Duncan on Vancouver Island. Oldtimers will remember the Bloedel, Stewart & Welch logging camp at Myrtle Point near Powell River at which this locie was used. The camp started in 1911 and when it finished operations in 1928, the Shay locie went to Menzies Bay and from there to Great Central Lake. When Great Central Lake camp shut down, the "One Spot", as it was known, was loaded on a barge and towed to Vancouver from whence it was to be sent to the Philippine Islands to continue its long and useful life. However, something went wrong with the deal and the importer was refused a permit. Jerry Wellburn, a logging machinery collector, had it transported to the forest museum he established and its old balloon stack will be on view for many, many years yet.

Cowichan Lake around 1923. This turn of logs destined for Selkirk Bridge, Victoria.

100

Early logging railway, 1908.

Old logging locie used at Crow's Nest Pass Lumber Company in 1921.

Climax locie at Otter Point, Vancouver Island, Sylvania Logging Company, 1918.

Old logging locie used at Crow's Nest Pass Lumber Company in 1921.

Early logging camp in B.C. woods. Between the two of them, steam donkey and steam locie, they gobbled up a tremendous amount of wood and time spent in cutting it. The job required a full time crew.

Elk River Timber Company's 70 ton Shay locomotive.

Comox Logging and Railway Company locomotive and large load of logs.

Another logging locie of interest was the "Six Spot" at Chemainus. This fifty-ton Shay carried 180 pounds of steam and was built by Lima Locomotive Works in Ohio in 1906. Unfortunately it was scrapped a few years ago. A happier fate awaited the big rod engine known as the "One Spot" at Cathel & Sorenson's railroad at Port Renfrew. It was whispered around the west coast that this locie was too big to stay on the track. It had been fitted already with counterweights to settle it down but remained in an old locomotive shed for many years until it was purchased by American-born John Humbird at Chemainus. It operated on the railway between Ladysmith and Nanaimo as the "1077" until 1970. At that time the British Columbia government bought the engine and it is now operating as part of a traveling museum.

Ladysmith Lumber Company Railway served a small sawmill in Cedar District using a locie known as the "Nanaimo." This little pot weighed ten tons and was brought around the Horn in a sailing ship from England in 1874. The machine was thrown on the scrap heap after some years of use but was resurrected in 1912 and its history continued. It was shipped to Squamish at one point to lay steel for the Pacific Great Eastern, working there until about 1915 under a "hogger," or engineer, named Angus McRay. Then it mysteriously disappeared.

Another old locomotive used on the Ladysmith Lumber Company Railway was of real interest as it was originally Number 168 of the New York Elevated Railway. It had a vacuum bellows to apply the brakes on the wheels and cottonwood brakeshoes. It hauled coal and logs for the Ladysmith company.

A little twelve ton locie that ran on the original railroad to East Wellington outside Nanaimo is now standing in Piper Park in that city. It was built in 1883 by the Baldwin Locomotive Works and arrived in the Hub City to haul timber and coal. A narrow gauge railway belonging to Eastern Lumber Company was a reconstruction of the original narrow gauge that ran from Crofton to Mount Sicker Mines near Duncan. When a little Shay overturned on that narrow gauge railway one day, killing the engineer, all logging railroads in British Columbia were ordered to become standard gauge.

Crown Zellerbach Canada is establishing a fine collection of old logging equipment and trees from various parts of the world at Ladysmith on Vancouver Island. This old beauty, a fifty ton Shay, and a Baldwin rod engine built in 1923, are on display there.

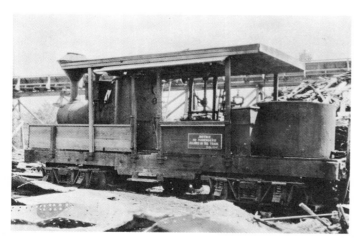

Oldtime locie used at Shawnigan Lake Logging.

Steam locomotive and crew of woodcutters working for Comox and Campbell Lake Timber Company. Photo taken by Leonard Frank, prominent pioneer photographer of British Columbia in September, 1919.

Coast logging locomotive number one at B.C. Mills, Timber & Trading Company, 1913. Notice the neat pile of cordwood.

At Jordan River, on the western shores of Vancouver Island, the Island Logging Company used Climaxes to haul logs to the beach for further transportation by raft. When the claim was taken over from Michigan Lumber Company in 1912, the organization inherited a fifty-ton Climax which was later sent to Rock Bay, but this old beauty was unfortunately scrapped at Franklin River in 1947.

105

The mystery of the disappearing locomotive. This little "pot" (engineer J.K. Hickman) weighed ten tons and came around the Horn from England in 1874. It disappeared around 1915 while laying steel for the P.G.E.

The first large logging show at San Juan on the west coast of Vancouver Island was staged by British Canadian Lumber Company, employer of more than one hundred men and operator of a four-mile railway from Fairy Lake to the mouth of Gordon River from 1912 to 1914. (Bert Davis, who invented the Davis raft, was superintendent there and his brother Otis was a locie engineer.) W.E. Cathels and C.S. Sorenson arrived in the area during the mid-Twenties and built a logging railroad along the south bank of the main branch of the San Juan River as far as the mouth of the Gordon River where they had their booming grounds. All the railroad construction was done by hand, pick, shovel and axe. The larger trees were hauled off the grade by a donkey engine, the first to be used at Port Renfrew. Eventually there were more than one hundred miles of track in the Port Renfrew area, and by 1950, British Columbia Forest Products had 300 miles of track there.

Climax locie used in logging on Vancouver Island now on display at British Columbia Forest Museum.

A 45 ton Climax logging in the Nimpkish Valley in 1928.

Big Climax that worked for Rat Portage Lumber Company Ltd. in Vancouver.

Locie No. 4 at Chemainus shop of Victoria Lumber and Manufacturing Co. Ltd. in September, 1940. A tender has just been installed and the locie hauled an extra car. Discussing whether or not two tenders would haul two extra cars are (left to right) Frank Work, Jack McKinnon, Harry Heslip and Bert Steele.

Built in 1883 by the Baldwin Locomotive Works, this old beauty came to East Wellington (Nanaimo area) to tote timber and coal. It's now in Piper Park in Nanaimo.

108

A 70 ton, three-truck Shay locomotive built at Lima Locomotive
Works in 1913. Reported to be first
delivered to a company in Eastern
Canada and later lost in St. Lawrence River. Was salvaged and purchased by Nimpkish Timber Company and put into service. A new
trailer was installed in 1929 and a
new frame in 1944 for use by Canadian Forest Products as switcher
at Woss and Vernon camps.

There are many stories about logging train derailments and wrecks;
incidents when engineers and brakemen bailed out after the brakes
failed to hold the charging locies and their trains of logs on steep
grades. One that drew more smiles than sighs was when the Rat
Portage Lumber Company's brand new seventy-ton Climax ran away.
The Climax had been put to work on that day in 1918 at the head of
Indian Arm on Burrard Inlet. Within hours it was speeding backwards,
driverless, towards the Inlet. It hit a stump, bounced, and dove straight
in, coming to rest in water up to the cab, the smoke stack slightly askew
but still puffing. It was dried out, returned to the track, working for
many years around Vancouver. Later it was taken to Vedder Crossing
near Chilliwack and from there to Englewood on northeastern Vancouver Island where it hauled logs until 1955.

As well as the few logging locomotives still surviving, there are a few
steam traction engines, reminders of a time when innovative loggers
used these prairie steamers to pull wagonloads of logs instead of
threshing machines. Some were still active in 1920 and a good example
of these engines is one known as a Waterloo which is displayed at
British Columbia Forest Museum.

Railroad men were loggers, too. Here the locie crew pose with the loaders and operators of the crane at Franklin River, sometime in the Fifties.

Canadian Forest Products, Englewood Division is one of the few locie shows left in British Columbia logging, but all-diesel now. Here's nostalgia: No. 29 Pacific Coast Shay and No. 4, a 70 ton Porter. Photo taken in 1955.

Wherever trains go, so go bridges—first—and some of the bridges connecting valley to valley were huge. The Bear Creek trestle on the west coast of Vancouver Island was about 250 feet high and 700 feet across. It was supported by three trusses each ninety feet long. The smaller San Juan trestle was 154 feet high, 600 feet long and was supported in the centre by an A-frame.

The last haul of logs by a steam locomotive in North America was on Monday, December 1, 1969, when Number 1055, a forty-one year-old Baldwin saddle tank steam locomotive hissed into Ladysmith railroad yard and ground to a stop. Owned by MacMillan Bloedel, old 1055 weighed only one hundred tons and generated 200 pounds of steam per square inch. On her last run, 1055 hauled thirty railway flatcars bearing about 2,000 tons of logs. Railway veteran Pete McGovern was at the throttle as engineer on 1055's last run across trestles spanning yawning canyons and around precipitous rock bluffs. It was a downhill run all the way, in more ways than one for the retiring engine. The sixteen-mile route from the logging camp to ocean level drops about

Salmon River Logging Company with 70 ton Climax.

110

Locie 1055 takes out the last load of logs at MacMillan Bloedel's Nanaimo River camp.

1,000 feet and with 2,000 tons of huge Douglas fir, cedar and hemlock logs resting on the flatcars, brakemen Ray Manning and Jack McAdam had their hands full to keep old 1055 from running wild during the two and one-half hour ride. This Baldwin locie had a checkered history. Built in Philadelphia in 1928, she hauled the forest harvest from many areas of Vancouver Island—first around Campbell River from about 1928 to 1940, later in the Port Alberni area. She ended her days as a logging locie at the MacMillan Bloedel Chemainus Logging Division. Her steam whistle on that day in 1969 heralded the end of an era. After fifty years of railroad logging, the timber was too far into the hills for most firms to build railroads to the mountain tops. Logging trucks now reign supreme on the coast.

Narrow gauge logging locomotive
used near Mission in Fraser Valley
in 1930's.

Locie No. 11 unloading logs at Ladysmith.

112

Old Curly would never believe this. Canadian Forest Product's diesel locomotive and cars of logs at Camp A, 1959.

It was bound to happen. By 1948 there were only sixteen logging railways left in British Columbia. In 1969 there were two. Now Englewood Division of Canadian Forest Products operates the only railroad-truck show in the province, and all the locies are diesel-powered. The reason for the decline in railroad logging is very simple: railroads had practical limits of five per cent grades and twenty degree curves; trucks can negotiate grades up to twenty per cent and sometimes take ninety degree curves.

Railroad buffs, even those who never saw a real logging locomotive and a train of logs in action, mourn the passing of the steam locies. But the men who really miss them most are the engineers, the brakemen, the firemen and the woodcutters. There was nothing quite like that steaming old chunk of steel, whistling through the forest, cab full of red hot pipes and vents and pressure gauges, the furnace gobbling wood or coal through a mouth of fire. Those early railroaders were a breed unto themselves, cantankerous as well as courageous. Men streaked with engine oil and soot, they wheeled their beloved machines over difficult terrain and impossible grades. One oldtimer tells the story of an engineer who accidentally mowed down the camp superintendent's pet dog with his locie. The super tore a strip off the engineer leaving him seething in silence. A couple of weeks later the engineer was wheeling down a grade when the fireman shouted: "There's a log on the tracks." Instead of braking, the engineer gave two toots and full throttle. The train plowed into the log and jumped the track. No one was seriously injured but the dazed superintendent was angry and demanded of the engineer why he had deliberately hit the log at full tilt. "Damn it!" the engineer said, "I thought you said there was another *dog* on the tracks!"

113

Hard-tired truck on a "fore and aft" road. The driver was unprotected except for the railroad ties between him and the load. This was in 1924.

8.

Trucking Down

From the fore and aft to the whole truck show.

The easiest way to start an argument between two oldtime truck loggers is to speculate when the first trucks were used to transport logs in the woods.

All cinched down and ready to go is this oldtimer. The driver has a tie-back for protection against his head. "Give them a little wind and they'd blow over," one driver complained. Note that a "strawline" cable has been wrapped around the truck's rear wheels to give added traction.

One thing is sure: the first logging trucks used on the British Columbia coast were solid-tired, cab-less and ran on "fore and aft" roads constructed of logs laid end to end. Locations too steep for railroading or not extensive enough to warrant their expense, were now about to be handled by the truck loggers. The location and date most mentioned by oldtimers when they talk about the first trucking venture is that of Forbes Bay at the mouth of Toba Inlet on Homfray Channel in 1924. Those Leyland trucks owned by Bob Campbell hauled on hewn lumber roads for the Forbes Bay Logging Company.

But trucker-inventor Archie McKone of Vancouver reported that the first real attempt to put trucks to work hauling logs was at Northern Pacific Logging Company at Loughborough Inlet in 1922-23. He should know; he was there.

Archie McKone, pioneer trucker and inventor, at wheel of famous old White truck restored to her original glory for Truck Loggers' Convention in Vancouver, 1942. The log was hauled from Granville Island to Georgia Street convention centre. Pictured are Norman English, Tom Murphy, Pat Maloney and Harry McQuillan, superintendent at Pioneer Timber.

The famous Archie McKone Truck Turntable at use on Malcolm Island 1936 for Pioneer Timber Company. Truck drove to end of pier and automatically turned around to face back up fore and aft road again. In picture (left to right) "Aussie" Holman, Archie McKone, Charlie Peterson, "Red" Manion. Last man is unidentified.

A railroad show, Northern Pacific Logging, utilized four trucks, all Whites, three brand new and one vintage 1918. McKone was hired by contractor Alf Mann of New Westminster to go to Loughborough with the new trucks which had been purchased in Seattle. They were outfitted with custom-built Universal five-ton trailers built by Pacific Car and Foundry at Renton, Washington. The 1918 White was already at the site. The new trailers had tires that matched the tread of the rear tires on the trucks: forty by fourteen inches. The front tires measured thirty-six by seven inches.

The last day of hard-tired logging trucks at Port Mc-Neill. Trucks used were Whites and of 1920s vintage. The bus, or crummy, in foreground was built by Archie McKone who took the photo.

"You had to drive darn carefully to keep the front tires on those old fore and aft roads," McKone said. The log "rails" were laid like railroad tracks, open in the centre except where stringers crosswise supported lengthwise logs. These two sixteen-inch wide tracks had squared saplings alongside for guard rails. McKone knows all about building these early timber roads, having become expert in shaping a ninety-foot tree as close as possible to sixteen inches all the way from butt to top with a scoring axe and broad axe. "The trouble was," McKone said, "not all those trees were cut that close to specifications and sometimes there'd be as much as six inches difference at the end where they lay on the cap and came up against the next sixteen-inch butt." Even by driving as close to the guard rail as possible, the driver still took a chance in bouncing off the "track" if the front wheel hit one of those protruding butts.

Oldtimers like this can be handled by youngtimers like this at British Columbia Forest Museum near Duncan on Vancouver Island.

Hauling poles at Bear Creek, near Chase, B.C. Drivers of these old trucks were "right on top of things" with no protection from shifting load except the horse-hair stuffed seat.

No identification on this photo of oldtime hard-tired truck and trailer loading lumber. From Roozeboom Collection at Provicial Archives.

Oldtimer Frank White described the experience of driving down those roads in a cab-less truck with hand brakes on the outside: "Sittin' out in the open on a board seat, a couple, three thousand foot of logs jigglin' around behind your head, no bulkhead for protection, that steering wheel just like a bull's hind leg in your hands . . . you were earnin' your two dollars and eighty cents a day."

With mud or frost on the road, the truck was harder to control than holding a greasy pig with one hand. But Archie McKone said the most dangerous part about driving with the old trucks was not the trucks themselves, but the loading procedures.

"They always wanted to cinch the logs to the frame and I was always against it. If the log rolled it usually took the truck and driver with it, like a dog wrestling with a bear. I never cinched my load unless the boss absolutely insisted on it," McKone said. (He was more often than not his own boss.) "I'm not like the sea captain who wanted to go down with his ship. I wanted to get off and drive again. The operators in those camps figured if you were out there in the elements you would have your mind on the job and be right there on top of things," McKone continued.

Some truckers made a bulkhead of railroad ties (called "tie backs") secured with U-bolts at top and bottom to form a buttress between load and driver. "A good wind would blow it over on you," McKone scoffed. He was at Koprino Harbor hauling balsam one spring when the bark skinned off the top log and it slid forward into the tie back. "It shoved me into the steering wheel and my feet flew off the pedals," McKone said. The truck picked up speed, out of control. Luckily a trailer wheel hit one of those infamous butt ends, twisted over and dropped its load. As the logs slid off, the tie back straightened enough so that McKone could reach his pedals and stop the truck. Despite some bad experiences like that, McKone, who drove his last load of logs for Crown Zellerbach at Courtenay in 1969 when he was seventy years old, liked driving the old trucks best.

Don't look now fellas, but . . . This suspended action shot took place at Comox Logging and Railway's operation at Ladysmith in 1937. Truck has makeshift cab with corrugated iron roof.

Comox Logging and Railway Company crew aboard old Leyland truck at Ladysmith in 1937.

119

"They had good ratcheted hand brakes and were geared so low you could pull up quite an adverse—say, twenty-eight to thirty per cent grade. Of course, you had to feel your brakes all the time. But it kept you on your toes."

Long logs being taken out by Alice Lake Logging Company during the 1940's.

His attitude was, "If you had a big log to move, you went ahead and moved it." He "moved it" a lot of times, some of them like an occasion at Kelsey Bay once, when he was driving an 848 Kenworth, belting down a steep incline, a log slipped off the load and over the top of the cab like a launched rocket. It slithered down the gravel in front of him but hit the ditch so he could drive on past without even stopping. The same thing happened twice more, and each time he and the truck escaped any collision with the falling logs.

This scene shows good view of "fore and aft" hewn log road leading under McLean or "hayrack" boom. Truck has hard tires: this one has a cab. Malcolm Island camp of Pioneer Timber Company.

Early Kenworth logging truck with large log cinched.

Highballing like that came naturally to McKone, was, in fact, a tradition with him. In 1936 he was called upon to log a claim at Malcolm Island where the fore and aft road was decaying and the logs had to be removed quickly before the road caved in completely. "Speed was the only answer," McKone said. "Averaging sixty loads a day, with nine trucks, we accounted for six million board feet in a month." There were no serious accidents, although one driverless truck slipped its brakes and ran straight as a die until a rear trailer wheel hit an abutment and it flipped over; the equipment was a write-off.

Coffee Break? This photo shows good detail of a plank road, this one at Port McNeill, Branch 10 of Pioneer Lumber Company, about one mile past Clux-ewe Crossing.

Crotch line with "L" hooks at Chase, B.C. See donkey mounted on back of old truck in front.

Truck logging at Veddar, B.C. Notice the plank road and truly huge load on truck.

Fancy meeting you here! Two oldtimers meet head-on on a logging road in the 1950's.

122

One of the reasons for all that good production was McKone's genius for improvisation. A natural inventor, he has been called a "real gyppo Thomas Edison" with a flair for making something out of nothing. Two of his gadgets were widely used in coast logging: a pre-loader for logging trucks and a truck turn-table, both patented devices. The McKone Pre-Loader eliminated loading delays. Trucks were provided with detachable "bunks" so loading crews could build a load on them while the truck was away unloading another set of detachable bunks. When the empty truck returned, the driver would leave off his bunks and back under the loaded ones. Twenty-six logging firms on the coast used the Pre-Loader manufactured in Vancouver. "The loading crews didn't like it much," McKone said. "It kept them too busy."

Archie McKone's Pre-Loader in operation at Northwest Bay Logging Co. Ltd. near Nanaimo. Boom lifts "bunks" off truck which driver then moves forward and backs under the load set up on extra set of bunks on right hand side.

The McKone Truck Turntable worked on the principle that what goes forward must come back. Utilizing its own motive power, the truck hooked onto a cable, the cable pulled on a drum, and the whole thing turned around. In one operation at Malcolm Island, the turntable, like part of the fore and aft road, was suspended on pilings about sixteen feet above the water. "You were up so high you felt like an eagle getting ready to set on a mulberry bush," McKone said. By the time a new driver got to the end of the turning table he was clawing at his throat and wondering if he was going to take a nosedive into the salt chuck. But by then the table had turned and the truck was facing up the road

123

Since the fore and aft roads were similar to a railway, vehicles could pass only at prepared passing "tracks". Each button on the dispatcher's board shown here represented a vehicle identified by truck number. As the drivers called in on telephones located at intervals along the road, Ben Gleason ("Old Ben") of Pioneer Timber Company in Port McNeill would move the marker along the board to advise the driver whether to proceed or hold on. The levers in front of Ben worked a number of signals in the dispatch shack which gave further instructions to the drivers.

The big one has the load! Comox Logging Company vehicle, crew and logs at Ladysmith in early 1940's. Men on load are Henry de Clarke (driver), Jim Sheasgreen, logging company manager, Vic Dodds, shop foreman, Hughie Cliffe, Ray Berod, mechanic or machinist, Joe Cliffe, foreman. One man is unidentified.

and ready to go back for another load. "The drivers got so much fun out of it they used to play around with it on Sundays like it was a toy," McKone said.

Another invention of McKone's, worked successfully at Pioneer Timber at Port McNeill, was his own version of vacuum brakes. But his favorite gadget wasn't marketed at all. It was a make-do radiator he devised for Charlie Gustafson at Koprino Logging Company in Quatsino Sound. "There were two cold decks to move and we were really highballing it when a log hit the truck's radiator and smashed it," McKone said. Gustafson wanted him to adapt a car radiator to the truck while waiting for a replacement to come from Vancouver but McKone said it was impossible. What was possible was to row to an abandoned cannery and salvage a gas tank from an old boat which he affixed to the side of the truck. Using tinsnips and soldering iron, he fitted hoses to the cylinder head and water pump and fashioned a plug to let hot water out through the bottom of the improvised radiator. By stopping and refilling with cold water and letting out the hot at a stream on the way to and from the log dump, and once more at the donkey engine, he and a swamper managed to keep the truck going almost non-stop during daylight hours. "Charlie liked it so well he kept us humping even after we got the new rad from Vancouver," McKone said. "It was the best improvising job of my career."

Industrial Timber Mills Ltd. Wardroper Creek cat and arch show, 1946.

125

It had to be to beat his trip-of-a-lifetime, when he drove a truck pushing a trailer and pulling a wagon with two horses in it all the way from Rosedale-Agassiz area to downtown New Westminster. The reason he pushed rather than pulled the Universal five-ton trailer was because of the twisty road that hugged the mountainous terrain around Vedder Crossing to Sumas, the route to the coast in those days. Two old teamsters, Ollie Stanhope and Jimmy Russell, rode in the open cab with McKone while their team of white horses rode on the truck behind them, drooling all the time down McKone's neck. In all, the caravan stretched about eighty feet. It took from daylight to dusk to drive the distance, about one hundred miles. "I wish I'd had a movie of that," he said.

The donkey, sled and all, being moved by predecessor to Canadian Forest Products at Nimpkish in the 1940's.

Cluxewe Crossing around 1948, Pioneer Timber Company, Branch 10, Port McNeill. The "haystack" crib constructed of balsam logs for which there was not much market then, kept setting under the weight of the structure and loads. As a consequence the running surface had to be continually jacked-up and additional logs introduced.

127

Top:
Archie McKone drove his last load of logs at Courtenay on Vancouver Island for Crown Zellerbach when he was 70 years old. "I made a bet I'd last that long," he said.

Left:
Truck with big logs at Canadian Forest Products, Englewood Division, Beaver Cove.

Right: Plank road belonging to Pioneer Timber Company, Port McNeill, Vancouver Island. Truck shown is heading for the log dump. The road is still in use except it is now double-width gravel surface.

Archie McKone, who with partner George Smith contracted out as many as twelve trucks at a time at locations from Port Renfrew to Menzies Bay, has the highest respect for Canadian-made off-highway trucks, which he rates best in the world. He also has high respect for the drivers, although the oldtime trucker gets the nod as hardest worker. "The topic in the bunkhouse was how many logs you got out that day," McKone said. "Boy, we sure beat those guys down the bay. Drivers today got it soft. Nowadays a guy with a diploma and an air ticket comes to work and can't even change a glad hand." (A glad hand is a coupling arrangement for air brakes, and water to cool the brakes.) He figures the best drivers were young men who learned by experience. "A guy would come in setting chokers or working the tongs and watch how the drivers did their job. They ended up being the best drivers of all."

Trucks contracting to MacMillan Bloedel log off into the sunset at Port McNeill.

Loading the supertruck. The frontend loader, in addition to putting the bite on the load, lifts the "pup" trailer when the truck and trailer are finished loading and places the trailer on the back of the truck for returning to the woods for another load.

Nevertheless, the time has arrived now when the truck and the truck driver are really in high gear as far as logging goes. Some of these new forest giants are capable of performing almost the whole operation.

"It's the biggest logging truck in the world but it looks more like a roller skate," said Cliff Burrows, co-designer of a super truck built for Butler Brothers of Saanich on Vancouver Island. The truck is long, low and designed to have the logs resting on top of the cab; it is a far cry from the old crocodiles described by Archie McKone which had no cabs at all. The Butler Brothers truck was conceived by company president Claude Butler. It was built in one year by six men at a cost of about $200 thousand, including funds for testing it. The largest truck on record prior to the Butler supertruck was built by Kenworth and carried a one hundred-ton load, with trailer. The Butler truck carries a 200-ton load with carrier. "More important," Burrows said, "our truck will carry one hundred tons without the trailer and that is important in the bush where maneuverability is limited."

The world's largest logging truck with "pup" trailer and combined load of more than two hundred tons of logs. The supertruck owned by Butler Brothers of Victoria can carry twice the load of any logging truck on the North American continent. It was likely to stay ahead; at publication time the company was planning to add another trailer.

A type of truck you hardly see anymore. This one worked for MacMillan Bloedel and Powell River Company at Copper Canyon, west of Chemainus on Vancouver Island.

The daub marks on the logs indicate where the logs came from, whose they are and other necessary information.

Trucks contracting to MacMillan Bloedel at Port McNeill. "The trucks are so good nowadays the drivers can do the work half asleep."

Now that's what I call logs! Two trucks take out some long ones.

Canadian Puget Sound truck at Jordan River.

Road-building for logging operations is a true art in itself. See this well-constructed route through precipitous terrain at Jordan River on Vancouver Island.

132

Log loader operator Bernie La-blanc maneuvers a heavy hem-lock into position on the waiting truck. In the background Paul Papso operates a Madill grapple yarder. The side is in the Kunnun area, about 14 miles from Mac-Millan Bloedel's Eve River dryland sort.

Off-highway log hauling for Rayon-ier. Notice the wide bunks.

Oldtime trucker Frank White of Gibsons, British Columbia, is con-temptuous of the new breed of truck and driver. "Half the guys don't even know what the brake pedal's hooked up to," he says. "There's just one guy to load you and it doesn't matter how he throws the logs on because you hardly notice they're there. They're all broomsticks anyway." White said today's trucks are so good the drivers can do the work half asleep. "The trucks never stop but the driver's so sloppy you don't get any more logs than we did before. It's like everything else. They've done away with the work—not the worker."

Whether the good old days were as good as they are today should give the oldtime truckers something else to argue about while they're dueling over where the first logging trucks were used in the Province.

133

Sunday was a time for fun and games at camp. Like falling chin whiskers and washing out the old socks and underwear in a tub of water heated on a campfire. The man being shaved looks like he's holding a prayer book, just in case the faller with the razor makes a miscalculation.

134

9.
The Way They Were
Camp life then and now.

If there is a single word to describe the few hours that men in the very early logging camps had for leisure, that word would be "boring."

In the late 1800s, long before radio or television, there were few newspapers, magazines, and books available. Nothing much relieved the monotony of the eat, work and sleep routine. Few members of the largely Scandinavian crew could read English and, besides, the only time available for reading was at day's end when flickering oil lamps were the only illumination in the bunkhouses. Mail was delivered on a haphazard basis, but the loggers moved so frequently that sometimes it took years for a letter to catch up to the man it was addressed to.

This group of early loggers in B.C. had a musician in their midst and had hopes of a song coming along. Men had to provide their own entertainment.

To pass the time, some men became skilled woodcarvers while others braided leather and rope into attractive works of art, a few examples of which can be seen today in family collections. Off-duty time was often spent sharpening axes and saws. But for many men, eating and sleeping were the only forms of entertainment. That and fighting, or watching other men fight. Boredom made it inevitable that the least triviality was reason enough for a fight. Sunday meant a break of sorts (although in many early camps Sunday was just another work day) and if it had stopped raining a logger could go for a swim to remove some of the caked-on grime; he could fish, hunt or swap lies with someone.

135

Gambling was a passion and many camps—in the era before camp recreation centres and ready access to nearby towns—were populated by single men with lots of money and nowhere to spend it. There were some wild poker games. The loggers had what they called a poker shack, usually a portion of one of the bunkhouses. In the Thirties it was nothing to see ten or fifteen thousand dollars change hands on a weekend.

An amateur barber could fall a few whiskers or cut somebody's hair, and they his. Others would wash their clothes in a big pot of water heated over an open fire. The main items were socks and—if it was spring—heavy underwear. The outer wear seldom got washed, and for a good reason. A logger's garb had to be practical. Pants got stiff from dirt and a combination of pitch from the trees, oil from the crosscut saws and grease from the skidroad. The pants could practically stand by themselves.

"Whenever I went to town I used to chuck my tin pants into the bush and leave them there until I came back," said oldtimer Charlie Hemson, who logged in the Cowichan Lake area in the 1880s.

These "tin pants" were also called "stag pants" or "stagged-off pants" and had no cuffs. Cuffs tended to get snagged or filled with chips and other woodland debris so the loggers cut them, sometimes with an axe. This aversion to cuffs continued and the practical logger of the 1940s still looked upon them as an affectation, good only for shaking cigarette ashes into if he happened to be caught in somebody's front parlor. Underwear was of the well-known, heavy woollen "longjohns" variety. The shirt was patched and worn and peppered with holes made by sharp twigs and saw teeth. A shapeless hat, woollen socks that were either full of holes or darned to death, and heavy soled shoes or boots completed the workaday outfit. Later on, caulk (pronounced "cork") boots studded with sharpened nails and steel tipped laces that inched up through a dozen holes and eyelets were introduced.

Shave and a haircut? I meant shave my beard, not my head! These boys were getting spruced up at the B.C. Forest Products camp at Cabin Creek in 1948. They're identified as timber cruisers, the men who make the inventories of forest stock.

The Hasting Camp near Campbell River on the east coast of Vancouver Island in 1896. Even the little boy on the right hand side of the picture has his hat on.

"Let's see now, on Sunday I guess we could clean up the front yard." Early camp in the Vancouver area had makeshift bunkhouses, some with tent roofs.

The eat, work, sleep syndrome was the way it was in early camps like this. At least the kids in front had a dog to play with.

If it was raining, and in the rain forests it rained as heavily then as now, the logger donned a jacket which he may have weather proofed with a mixture of wax and kerosene. Later versions of this jacket were manufactured and called by various names, the more printable ones being duckbacks, drybacks and bonedrys. At first they were little more than pieces of canvas with arm holes that were brought together with steel snap buttons at the front. Later manufacturers put a thin sheet of rubber between two layers of canvas. The result was both a joy and a curse to the workingman. Designed to keep him dry, the canvas-rubber combination also contained his sweat so the logger was almost always wet regardless of whether or not it was raining. As one good-humored old Swede put it: "No matter how cold and vet you got, you vere alvays varm and dry."

Fallers ignored the jackets completely. Theirs was a balancing act already: what with trying to stand on a springboard four to six feet off the ground and swinging a one-pound, double-bitted axe with a forty-two inch handle through a gaping undercut, they would not also contend with a stiff bag of canvas across their shoulders. "What we did was to wear two Stanfield shirts," said oldtime faller Bus Griffiths of Fanny Bay on Vancouver Island. "We wore the one shirt inside our pants and the other one—which we boiled in hot water and linseed oil so it shrunk up tight like a horse blanket—hung on the outside. If it got real wet we reached around once in a while and wrung out the tail. And if it got really soaked, well, we just had to get down and take the top shirt off and wring it out and put it back on again."

To make up for these unfortunate working and living conditions, camp bosses strove to put good food on the table because a logger would suffer almost anything except bad food. And he had an appetite that matched his work output. Asked if it was true that they ate eight eggs with their breakfast steak, Texada Islander Don Tweedshope replied: "Not that I know of, but occasionally we'd eat a whole leg of lamb or two." Finding and keeping good cooks and their flunkey helpers wasn't an easy job, despite the fact that cooks were paid almost as much as fallers.

137

Bernard Timber and Logging Company at Port Neville in 1926.

Victoria Lumber and Manufacturing Company, Camp 10 at Cowichan Lake, 1926.

Raft camp, or float camp, at Sandspit. The interesting part of this photo is the fact that the far end of the camp bunkhouse was part of an old North Vancouver ferry. This was J. Gordon Gibson's camp in 1945. Gibson's quarters were in house at near end.

Part of the crew at Weatherhead's camp at Yahk, B.C. in 1925. Yahk is a small community between Creston and Cranbrook.

Royal City Mill logging camp at Mud Bay on Hall's Prairie Road south of Cloverdale heading towards American border. Notice the man on right is on crutches. Light duty on woodpile today?

Not all logging camps were on ground. In fact, many were on floats like this one near Echo Bay.

Dunning Hoff of Fort St. James started his logging career as a teen-aged flunkey for fifty dollars a month at Fort Garry Lumber Company when that Winnipeg firm had a camp twenty-five miles west of Prince George on the Canadian National Railway line. It was 1926. Everything in the bunkhouse, machine shop and cookshack was made from logs except the lumber in the roofs and floors which was cut on the scene.

There were no ceilings, just a crisscross of rafters and beams. "That left lots of room for rotten socks to hang from," Hoff said. It was typical for the times.

In the very early days men slept in bunks tiered four high which were "muzzle-loaded". That is, the weary logger had to crawl up to his appointed sack through the end of the bunk. In Hoff's time thirty men in double bunks slept in a bunkhouse warmed by a big McClary potbellied stove that was kept going day and night in fall and winter with wood cut by an energetic bullcook whose other jobs included sweeping out the buildings and—sometimes—making beds. The room, with windows high up in the gable at either end, was lit at dusk by two Coleman gas lanterns and each bunk had a kerosene lamp above it to allow the occupants to read, play cards or file an axe by its flickering, smoking glimmer. Camp orders were that all lights were to be doused sharp at nine. But Hoff, the flunkey, was in the kip as early as five-thirty, while some loggers were still eating dinner, or "supper" as it was more commonly known. He had to be up just after three in the morning to begin peeling a fifty-pound lard pail full of potatoes. If he was lucky and the cook was in a good humor, he'd get a cup of coffee early on. Otherwise he'd have to wait until after breakfast when the loggers had departed for the woods.

Skidding logs by sleigh in the spring of 1943 by Chief Lake camp of C. B. Hoff Sawmill. Dunning Hoff is driver.

"If you got a good cook you could get cleaned up and finished early, otherwise you never got done working." Spotless cookshack at Brooks, Scanlon & O'Brian camp at Stillwater, 1926.

139

"Some were sloppy guys who were easy to get along with but you never got done working. You just got breakfast served and the dishes put back clean on the tables and you had to start all over again. Then it was clean up and get ready and serve and clean up again. Sometimes it was better to work with a cranky cook who was efficient because you got done early."

In the Forties some camps were trying out girl flunkeys. Women cooks had been around for some time but they stayed in the kitchen and girl flunkeys were close enough to touch—if you dared. Loggers who used to come to the table looking like the wrath of God now washed for meals and at supper time showed up in white shirts, open at the neck, but reasonably clean. Their language had cleaned up considerably, too, but there were problems.

The camp superintendent at Bloedel's on Great Central Lake painted a yellow line across the float camp decking next to the girl's quarters making the area off limit to the loggers after lights out. This didn't make him any more popular than he was already but, overall, the presence of women had a salutary effect on the men's morale. That is, they were still frustrated, but they were smiling more.

"I owe my soul to the company store." Gus Johnson and Al Kalberg man the counters where loggers could buy clothing, tobacco and other necessities.

"Jap Town" at Ocean Falls, February, 1942. The Japanese who worked at Pacific Mills were given separate accommodation from "white" workers. During the war they were moved from here and white workers moved in. The author lived in one of these houses in July, 1950. The smoke behind is from the pulp digesters. Mill is now government controlled.

Some loggers preferred the quiet off-duty life—some still do—to the more
frantic life of the urban dweller. Here Tom McPherson relaxes in his Nimpkish
bunkhouse room in 1955. Room had two occupants.

Forging 120 pound loading tongs are blacksmith Steve Machibroda (holding
tongs) and Einer Vikback with sledge hammer. The loggers at Pioneer Lumber
Company at Port McNeill referred to these giant tongs as the "Peck Specials"
after Bert Peck, superintendent at the time. "For his money anything lighter
wouldn't stand up," they said.

141

Serving up time at Pioneer Timber Company, Port MacNeill, 1946. Pictured are head cook George Blue and second cook Hugh Morrow.

In the Fifties and Sixties the logging camp cookhouse remained a place where eating was a deadly serious business. Although cookhouses had dwindled in number because of the trend to integration of loggers into community life, there were still many around and the early customs and rituals prevailed. Small talk at the table was discouraged. (This was particularly true in the early days when there were so many different languages spoken that if the men were allowed free reign to talk, dinnertime would have been like a fight in a henhouse.) Each man took the place assigned to him by the bullcook. Few men ever attempted to overrule the bullcook's decision, and to sit in another man's place was to court disaster. Good eating spots, like the best bunks, were usually earned through seniority. If the food wasn't served cafeteria style or at the table by the flunkey, it was left in dishes at the end of each table for the men to help themselves and then to pass down the line. You always asked politely for whatever you wanted. One man wanted some pie which was on the leeside of George Haywood's brawny arm. "He fired across my bow to get it and I rammed my fork into the back of his hand," Haywood recalled. "We had a little set-to right there on the floor. The next time he wanted something he asked for it properly."

George Lutz, now railroad superintendent at Canadian Forest Products' Englewood Division, recalls how he was frozen out of food altogether at one old camp. "I nearly starved to death where I sat," he said. "Every plate would be empty by the time it got to me. They were doing it on purpose because I was a new guy so one day I just slammed everything down and walked out."

No food served anywhere in the world surpasses that offered to loggers living in camp. A cook had to be on his toes or there'd be mutiny in the cookshack. Here a baker at Holberg camp on Vancouver Island takes out the bread. Picture was taken around 1950 but baker was unidentified.

Women, children, homelife and all the other amenities are available to loggers who live in or near communities today. This is Queen Charlotte City with residents.

Rarely does anybody slam down tools and walk out of today's modern cook shacks. The facilities are clean and the cooks and flunkeys are neat and polite. And in contrast to the beef and bean menu of a half century ago, here is a typical menu in today's camps:

Breakfast: Orange and applecot juice; rolled oats and dry cereal; stewed figs and prunes; soft boiled eggs; grilled minute steaks; bacon and fried eggs; hotcakes with syrup; toast with jam, honey or marmalade; coffee or milk.

Lunch: Beef and vegetable broth; grilled sirloin steak; creamed mushroom sauce; cold plate with egg salad; tossed assorted greens; baked potato and green peas or carrots; jello with fruit; deep apple pie; tea, coffee or milk.

Supper: Choice of juices; roast beef with gravy; deep fried prawns with rice; sardines on lettuce; red cabbage salad or cole slaw; scalloped potatoes; buttered green vegetables; donuts, cookies, fresh fruit, ice cream; coffee, tea or milk.

143

Not all logging camps were on land. This one at Holberg was once considered to the largest float camp on the coast.

Industrial Timber Mills Ltd. Nitinat Camp, near Lake Cowichan in the 1940's.

Honeymoon Bay as it looked in 1948.

Holberg on Vancouver Island is a "Rayonier Town" but it's not at all like the company towns of the early days. More settled now, loggers take an interest in community events and services.

Now hear this! . . . a safety meeting for all residents at Woss Camp in 1956.

On Sunday there's a "brunch" which usually features some treat like French toast or English muffins. It's served at ten o'clock for those who care to get up at that early hour. Many don't. They may catch some coffee and toast later at the Commissary.

The Second World War changed the look of things for most camps. Many of the residential camps on Vancouver Island closed down as road access into logging areas improved. The new breed of logger preferred to live in the nearby communities and commute back and forth daily to work. Some married men live in camp all week and go home on weekends. But for the logger who has to live in camp, life isn't too bad. He can read his mail, pick up a daily newspaper or magazine, go for a swim (some large camps have heated pools), shoot a game of billiards, phone his wife or girlfriend, wash his car, listen to a ball game on radio or see it on color television. If he wishes to be alone, he's got the wonderful world of the outdoors and he can fish or hunt, in season.

There's no reason for boredom anymore.

Man . . . camp life was never like this! The girls are fashion models from Vancouver who came up to the Holberg Camp of Rayonier for a show of the latest. The loggers and their wives approved.

145

A lonely day could be spent cutting up one of these big trees with a crosscut. Sometimes there was another man on the other end. One ingenious handlogger used to tie one end of his saw to a sapling with a rubber band and let it take the place of the "other guy."

146

10.
All Fall Down
The crosscut meets the powersaw and the woods are changed forever.

Pioneer loggers who used handsaws and double-bitted axes used to holler an exuberant *TIMBER*! to protect their fellow workmen from being struck by falling trees. Al Green, a Crown Zellerbach faller at Nitinat said, "If we hollered timber every time we downed a tree today we'd have a mighty hoarse throat by the end of the day. In the days of handsaws it wasn't always apparent to other men in the woods that a tree was being felled. Today the sound of the powersaw can be heard for several miles."

This early electric powersaw needed two men and a generator from a truck to operate it.

It's a sound now heard around the world, but the early powersaws were not exactly the efficient machines that we see and hear today. For example, there was one machine invented that cut through the tree by heat friction. This rope saw was developed from fine, two-way cutting steel. Attached to a cable and a double drum, the rope was run rapidly back and forth from one drum to the other, cutting through the tree in passing. It took several men a lot of time to set it up for use for each tree being cut.

147

One of the first chain saws to be used in B.C. Man with hat is Fred Espley and scene is Great Central Lake.

Sprightly seventy-year-old Gordie Willoughby repairs chainsaws at Jordan River for Canadian Puget Sound Logging.

Another variety used a red hot, electrically charged wire to fall trees by burning through the wood. The inventors of burning hot saws obviously weren't aware of the dangers of using such flammable items in tinder-dry woods. Other inventors had a seemingly endless supply of ideas. A device consisting of a series of augers which cut into the tree below ground level, thus eliminating stumps, was at least discussed, if not developed. A power faller was developed which had a long roller equipped with cutting teeth mounted on the end of a driven shaft. It could swing in a horizontal arc and could eventually cut its way through a tree. Electrical saws were being invented elsewhere. The Russians designed an electrical circular saw which was mounted on the front of a carriage. The saw was fairly light but the carriage was awkward to move from place to place. The English entered the race for the best saw design with a steam-driven drag saw for falling and bucking. The steam boiler was mounted on wheels and was drawn by horses while the saw portion was carried by hand. The difficulty of using such a saw on a sidehill show in British Columbia can readily be seen: the faller weighed six hundred pounds, without including the boiler or the bucking outfit.

"And this part is the rope you pull to start it." Crown Zellerbach loggers get instructions how to use the new-fangled machine.

Operating the old giant-sized powersaws was hard work. Crown Zellerbach field instruction.

149

Two-man powersaw of early variety that was a "kill-er" on the man as well as on the tree. They weighed up to 140 pounds and even carrying them through the bush was an effort.

They don't yell TIMBERRR! any more, but they still run. "I've had only shadows fall on me," one logger said, "but I ran just like it was a tree."

Obviously, none of these early devices were even remotely practical for use in the rough terrain of the Douglas Fir region. Between 1930 and 1935 several types of portable chain saws powered by two-cycle, high-speed motors were invented. The motors were unreliable and frequently failed, not only an annoyance but dangerous if the power failure came in the middle of falling a big tree. Nonetheless, these inventions were the forerunners of today's power saws.

By 1936, out of the welter of types and designs of portable saws, there emerged two definite contenders: the drag saw and the chain saw. The drag saw was successfully used in the California Redwoods where the size of the trees justified the necessity of constructing a platform on which the heavy, cumbersome saw could be set. The first two power-driven chain saws to be marketed in North America were the Wolf Saw, a very lightweight machine that could be driven by compressed air, electricity or gasoline motor; the Dow Saw was a heavy, awkward machine mounted on two rubber-tired wheels. Nevertheless, at a demonstration at Stirling City, California, on October 16, 1933, an "expert" pair of hand fallers and buckers lost out to the Dow Saw which cut a thirty-seven inch log in one minute and fifteen seconds, one-third of the time taken by the manual sawyers.

"Look, Ma, one hand!" Today's power saws can be operated by one man and the faller also bucks up the trees he cuts down.

Checking the decibel level on the powersaw. The saws have mufflers on them but there is still a lot of noise generated and hearing problems are high among loggers in the falling business.

The invention of the chain saw and its widespread use in British Columbia changed the face of logging. Gone were the old crosscuts; the music of the "Swedish Fiddle" was stilled forever.

151

John Ulinder, bullbucker at Copper Canyon for many years, scales this big fir which was one of many logs donated to the Osaka Pavilion at Expo '70.

Large Sitka spruce is bucked at MacMillan Bloedel's Queen Charlotte Division.

Even the undercut is made with the chain saw now.

Not since the advent of the steam donkey into the woods in the 1890's, was there such a change as that generated by introduction of the power saw.

John T. Pickles of Hebden Bridge, in England, developed a fairly practical gas chain saw that came in thirty, forty and sixty-inch sizes. A feature of the "Lynx" was the adjustability of the saw track to various setting positions. While the chain saw proponents seemed to have a definite edge on the market, E.J. Windle of Portland, Oregon, developed a lightweight drag saw called "The Little Giant" which looked exactly like a crosscut saw with a motor on top.

Meanwhile, back in British Columbia, men began lugging around the various products of Industrial Engineering Ltd., the Spear & Jackson and "The Hitler Machine," the Stihl Saw, built here under the name of Brunette. It had a five-foot bar, weighed about 140 pounds, and required two men in its operation.

Nowadays there are dozens of manufacturers with as many varieties of saws from which logging companies may choose, and further innovations are being tested in the province's forests. In 1970 Northwood Pulp and Timber Ltd. brought the first automatic feller to appear in the Prince George area, a giant tractor-mounted shear. The shear can pinch off a thirty-six inch diameter tree in just four seconds, but problems were encountered in the initial experiments because log butts were damaged by the pinching action of the shears. In October 1971, a tractor-mounted powersaw was tried out by Northwood and proved more successful. It can cut through a thirty-inch diameter tree in seven seconds without causing any damage to the butt.

It is believed by some that Jack Challenger introduced the chainsaw at Franklin River, but other sources contend "Gunny" Brown and Al Brown at Great Central Lake were the pioneers. Whoever deserves the credit introduced into British Columbia's logging the most important contribution to faster utilization of forest resources. Two fallers and a good bucker using a "Swedish Fiddle" produced 50 thousand cubic feet in 1934. With a chainsaw today, one man can fall and buck seventy-five to eighty thousand cubic feet in one eight-hour shift.

And without once having to yell *Timberrr!*

153

Highrigger prepares to climb the long, lonely way to the top of this giant spruce.

11.
Two of the Giants
Big trees from little acorns grow.

To study the background of the twelve giant forest conglomerates operating in British Columbia is to walk through the history of the logging industry.

Historic names appear and disappear, ever-changing and adapting like the forests themselves. Some fell to the bigger giants the way the trees fell before them: some healthy and protesting, others infested with rot, tottering with every wind, burnt-out or over-ripe, taking up space where new growth was required. The trend towards company amalgamation, mergers, take-overs and acquisitions had its start in the Depression years when small loggers and sawmills had difficulty hanging on financially. Joint-ownership of mill and camp increased during World War II and the consequent post-war prosperity. These factors, along with the insatiable lumber markets in Canada and United States brought about the emergence of the Giants: MacMillan Bloedel, British Columbia Forest Products, Rayonier, Crown Zellerbach, Canadian Cellulose, Canadian Forest Products, Weyerhaeuser, Northwood, Weldwood, Seaboard, Eurocan and Tahsis.

The objective of the great mergers was to make more profit by full utilization of inter-mixed timber holdings. These giant companies with unlimited capital, controlling every kind of forest products plant, could now drop all inefficient units and control every facet of the industry in order that maximum efficiency could be attained. This resulted in the logging camp, sawmill, veneer and plywood mill and pulp and paper mill becoming complementary to each other. The venture demanded enormous amounts of capital supplies largely by American corporations with—later on—more coming from Britain, Japan and Scandinavia.

155

H.R. MacMillan, from door-slammer to forest industry giant.

Two of the acorns who became forest giants were H.R. MacMillan, one of the founders of MacMillan Bloedel, and J. Gordon Gibson, formerly of Tahsis Company. H. R. MacMillan first saw British Columbia in 1907 when he arrived to survey coastal timber areas in Toba Inlet. As a young Canadian forestry graduate of Yale University he had first come to the attention of the Federal Government in Ottawa where he became Assistant Director of Forestry. He returned to British Columbia in 1912 at the request of the Provincial Government to found the British Columbia Forest Service and to become its first Chief Forester. World War I intervened and MacMillan was called in 1915 to serve with the Federal Government as a special Trade Commissioner to find lumber supplies for the British Government's war effort and to assess the capacity of the Canadian industry to supply these demands. He did not return to the Forest Service after that tour of duty but accepted a position as Assistant Manager of Victoria Lumber and Manufacturing Company at Chemainus. He did not stay long. In fact, he was fired. And as he was walking out of the door of the manager's office, he turned and said: "When I come through this door again, I'll own this blankety-blank outfit." Twenty-nine years later, in 1946, he did acquire the company and ordered the old battered door to be found and re-hung so he could walk through it and fulfill his prophecy.

Loading lumber on the J.V. Clyne at Harmac, near Nanaimo.

After the Chemainus incident, MacMillan went back to take another assignment for the Allied governments, this time as Assistant Director of the Imperial Munitions Board with the task of expediting production of airplane spruce for the air forces. At the end of the war he founded his own company, H.R. MacMillan Export Company with all his personal assets including "My house furnishings, and I wasn't too sure how long those would remain mine."

The company started its life as a sales agency selling British Columbia lumber in foreign markets. It owned no stands of timber, no timber mills, no logging camps and less than ten thousand dollars in assets.

Today it is the largest forest industry firm in Canada and one of the largest in the World. From the start the new company conducted a vigorous sales campaign for export markets; MacMillan, with another former forester and friend, W.J. VanDusen, travelled the world to search out customers. They found a receptive market in the United Kingdom and in the early 1920s concluded huge sales of railroad ties to India. The 1923 earthquake in Japan created a tremendous demand for lumber and the company served the market well, laying the foundations for what is today a thriving trade in the Far East. In order to ensure cargo space required to fill orders from the Orient, the export company formed Canadian Transport Company Limited as its wholly-owned subsidiary.

With MacMillan's firm the only Canadian company to be involved in such extensive worldwide trade, it is not difficult to understand the emotion with which he leaped to his feet at a world trade conference in Versailles after a delegate referred to Canada as an underdeveloped nation. "If Canada is underdeveloped, so is Brigitte Bardot," Mac-Millan said hotly. Mlle. Bardot was then at the full extent of her fame in France.

"City of Albernia" carrying a wartime lumber cargo under full sail to Australia. The last great voyage of a windjammer marked the end of an era and the transition from sail and steam to diesel-powered bulk carriers. With 40 ships under charter, Canadian Transport Company, a MacMillan Bloedel subsidiary, will carry 2.5 million tons of forest products and close to eight million tons of other dry bulk cargoes to ports throughout the world.

Bloedel, Stewart & Welch, Myrtle Point, 1926. This famous logging firm began operations in British Columbia in 1911.

In 1936 MacMillan began to produce lumber. His first purchase was the old Dominion Mills on the Fraser River, followed by Alberni-Pacific Lumber Company, descendant of the old Anderson Mill at Port Alberni which started production in 1861. He bought timber from the J.D. Rockefeller interests situated close to the Alberni-Pacific operations and this gave the organization a needed grip on lumber production. In 1940 the Campbell River Timber Company's timber was acquired, making MacMillan one of the three largest timber holders in British Columbia.

157

By 1946 the postwar prosperity enabled MacMillan to purchase the big Victoria Lumber and Manufacturing Company sawmill at Chemainus, the company from which he had been fired. Another historic event was in 1951 when MacMillan merged his company with Bloedel, Stewart and Welch. Both companies were major lumber producers at the time and their expanding units were operating literally next door to each other in the Port Alberni area. It was the largest consolidation of its kind in the industry in Canada at that time.

The story of Bloedel, Stewart and Welch in large measure centres around J.H. Bloedel, a name associated with the history of the Pacific Northwest since 1896. In the early 1900s, Bloedel, senior partner in the Washington state firm of Bloedel, Donovan, saw the great untapped softwood forests of British Columbia as an attractive prospect for his company. He joined forces with two Vancouver construction men to launch a new firm in 1911. These partners were Jack Stewart and Patrick Welch, original contractors for the Pacific Great Eastern Railway, now known as the British Columbia Railway, the major north-south rail link in the Province. In July, 1911, the firm of Bloedel, Stewart and Welch began logging operations at Myrtle Point on the Lower Mainland. The company confined itself to logging activities during its formative years and did not enter the manufacturing field until 1923 when it acquired Red Band Cedar Mill on the Fraser River near New Westminster. Two years later the company built a sawmill at Great Central Lake in the Port Alberni area, followed shortly afterwards by another on the Somass River which today is a key operating unit in MacMillan Bloedel's Port Alberni complex.

One of the first mobile spar trees to be used in British Columbia. The tractor-mounted donkey yarded the logs in from 200 to 300 yards with ease.

Brooks, Scanlon & O'Brian booming operation at Stillwater in 1926. This pioneer firm's founders were the nuclei of Powell River Paper Company which MacMillan merged with his firm to found the largest forest company in Canada and one of the largest in world.

158

Nanoose Carrier, *one of MacMillan Bloedel's newsprint barges under tow from Powell River.*

Faller Tom Weaver drops a big spruce at MacMillan Bloedel's Queen Charlotte Division.

At this time the company also acquired large blocks of Vancouver Island forests, including the Hill-Quinn tracts in 1927, which gave Bloedel, Stewart and Welch one of the largest forest reserves of any company in British Columbia. The company opened its Franklin River logging camp on Alberni Inlet in 1934, eventually becoming one of the largest single logging operations in the world, and one of the most advanced. It was at Franklin River that the Canadian forest industry saw its first steel spar in 1935 and the first chainsaw in 1936.

Another major event in MacMillan Bloedel's history came in 1959 when the Powell River Paper Company merged with the firm to form Mac-Millan, Bloedel and Powell River Company, a name now shortened to MacMillan Bloedel. The original founders of the Powell River Paper Company were the Brooks-Scanlon interests, American lumbermen. Under the name of Brooks-Scanlon-O'Brian, the firm began logging operations at Stillwater, British Columbia, in 1908 but Dwight Brooks and M.J. Scanlon saw in the nearby Powell River area an ideal site for a newsprint mill. A few years prior to the arrival of Brooks and Scanlon, the Provincial Government had issued a series of pulp leases to encourage development of a new industry. One of these, the Powell River lease, was held by Canadian Industrial Company and involved about 135,000 acres of prime timber. But the water rights to Powell Lake from which the mill's power would have to come were owned by Pacific Coast Power Company; these two firms merged and offered their properties and water rights for sale in 1909. Brooks and Scanlon were successful bidders and that same year incorporated Powell River Paper Company with a capital of $1,000,000. The plant turned out British Columbia's first roll of newsprint in April, 1912. Today Powell River can produce more than 1,800 tons of newsprint daily and is believed to be the largest single paper mill in the world.

159

In a major move toward integration, the Powell River company acquired the sawmill plants and properties of British Columbia Manufacturing Company at New Westminster in 1951 and also gained substantial reserves of timber. Martin Paper Products, a private company, was added and marked entry of the company into the corrugated container business with three plants on the Prairies and a fourth built in 1956 on Annacis Island in New Westminster.

But H.R. MacMillan didn't get to the top of the heap without problems. In 1935 a group of lumber producers representing nearly eighty per cent of the lumber production of British Columbia formed their own sales company and dispensed with H.R. MacMillan Export Company as their selling agent. The ensuing struggle for survival ultimately became a classic battle in the colorful history of the forest industry as the business community viewed it as the beginning of the end for H.R. MacMillan Export Company. MacMillan responded with characteristic vigor, however, and emerged stronger than ever.

H.R. MacMillan *loading pulp for delivery to ports around the world. MacMillan Bloedel owns many subsidiaries in United States and United Kingdom.*

Skagit Lumber Carrier at MB's Chemainus Sawmill Division. It was at this mill that H.R. MacMillan slammed a door that was heard around the world.

MacMillan Bloedel, aware that forest resources must be renewed, pioneered reforestation in British Columbia as early as 1938. The company has one of the highest allowable annual timber harvests in North America due to its intensive forestry management programs. MB brand products are sold in more than fifty countries; the company has many subsidiaries across Canada, in United States and in various other parts of the world from Britain to the Far East. The company employs about 20,000 people in North America. In British Columbia alone it has thirty logging divisions, four pulp and paper plants, shingle, plywood, particleboard and packaging operations. Fifteen mills in the United States produce both primary and secondary forest products. A complex of three mills in Alabama and twelve corrugated shipping container plants service regional U.S. markets from New Jersey to California. MB has five corrugated shipping container plants in the United Kingdom, an interest in paper mills in Holland, Belgium and Spain and an interest in a forest products operation in Malaysia. It also has other interests in Australia, Singapore and Indonesia.

160

H.R. MacMillan has come a long way since he slammed that door back in 1917.

Another man who has gone a long way in British Columbia's forest industry is J. Gordon Gibson, self-styled diamond-in-the-rough, the "Millionaire Gyppo".

Gibson, cigar-chewing iconoclast, believes every man in good health has the same opportunity to make a success, even in today's world. "We have nothing to fear from competition," he said. "We compete only against ourselves, not other people." Unlike MacMillan who had extensive formal education, Gibson was the ultimate drop-out. "I didn't drop out of university. I didn't drop out of high school. I dropped out of elementary school," he said. "Actually, I was thrown out after Grade Five. They didn't call us retarded in those days. They just called us dumb." Gibson, who founded Tahsis Company Limited with his father, W.F. Gibson, and three brothers, Clarke, Jack and Earson, said he wasted those five years in school but "I learned so little I have no trouble remembering it all."

A 988 "cat" unloads a truck in this typical scene at MB's Eve River Division dryland sort. In background a Dart log stacker prepares to lift a load and a D7 cat cleans up the sorting ground. More and more logging of this type is being done on land to prevent pollution of waterways.

Dart Log Stacker operated by Maurice Lamontaign of MacMillan Bloedel's Eve River Division drops a load of logs into the bundling rig. Bundled logs are rafted to booming grounds.

This magnificent stand of trees is known as Cathedral Grove and is a gift by H.R. MacMillan to the Province of B.C. Thousands of people visit the setting every year on the highway from Parksville to Port Alberni.

He may not have learned much, but he certainly applied his knowledge well. He started work at twelve, helping his father take out ship's knees at Parksville on Vancouver Island. The "knees" (timber with two arms connecting vessel's beams to frames) were used in construction of the *Malahat* and the *Tolmie*, two five-masted, bald-headed schooners in Victoria shipyards. From cutting knees for them, Gibson went on to own both those ships. So much for humble beginnings.

But that was later. The senior Gibson got a contract to provide Sitka spruce for the British air force and when the war ended they still had a lot of spruce on hand. With another contract, Gibson senior built a small sawmill at Ahousat on the west coast of Vancouver Island, outfitting it with an old, ninety-pound pressure steam threshing machine engine from the Prairies. That was in 1919 and times were tough and markets poor. They managed somehow to purchase an old second-hand shingle machine, then three more and some boilers and began to ship products to Vancouver. "Freight costs on the CPR *Maquinna* took almost half the selling price of lumber and shingles," Gibson said. The raw material was hand-logged off the property. At first it was all brute force with nothing more than the logger's usual aids: saw, wedges, axe and oil can. Then they acquired a team of horses. The first week the team strayed into some poisonous vegetation and one died of bloat. The remaining horse was unable to pull the logs alone so Gibsons traded it for two bulls which Gordon drove for a month. "But they were from the same herd and were always fighting with each other," he said. "The young bull almost killed the old one so he had to be shot. That was our salt meat for a couple of months."

J. Gordon Gibson, "The Millionaire Gyppo." Self-made businessman and former Member of the Legislature, Gibson said: "I've been called everything but lazy."

Father and sons in rare photo. W. F. Gibson in center flanked by sons Clarke, Jack, Earson and (extreme right) Gordon.

162

Typical loading scene in days when schooners like this took lumber to ports around the around the world. Gordon Gibson, and then others, acquired old sailing ships and converted their hulls into log barges.

J. Gordon Gibson (left) with mill superintendent Al Ramsey stand by as first log prepares its entry into Tahsis Mill in 1945. Tahsis Co. Ltd. was formed two years later.

They acquired a single-cylinder coal oil engine with 400 feet of three-quarter inch line and, with the remaining bull pulling the line into the woods and helping pull the logs back out, they made do until able to afford a small steam donkey. But their troubles were not yet over. A winter storm upset the A-frame on which the donkey was set; it took three months to raise it and put it back in service. In order to keep producing logs, they loaded their fifty-foot boat powered by a twenty-horsepower motor with heavy rocks, backed it into the area where trees had been felled with their tops almost in the water, ran out about 250 feet of three-quarter inch cable and then, with full speed ahead, jerked or pulled the trees into the water.

Using such ingenuity to overcome problems continued and during the next few years the Gibsons mixed fishing with logging until the big change in their lives came in 1934. That was when they bought that first five-masted schooner, the *Malahat*, sight unseen, for $2,500. "She had more than that in oil in her," Gibson said. The *Malahat*, fresh from her duties as mothership to rum-runners outside the twelve-mile limit off the California coast during Prohibition, came to load logs at Prince Rupert. But her equipment was not heavy enough so she returned "light" to Vancouver where a lien was placed against her for $2,500. The Gibsons wanted only the motor at first, as they planned to use its components as spare parts for a similar motor they owned; when they saw what they had bought they decided to get into world trade with her. In this they failed, but Tom Kelly, a Queen Charlotte Islands logger, told the Gibsons he'd pay five dollars for every thousand feet of logs they could deliver to the market. Gordon rounded up a crew of seventeen, composed almost equally of ex-rumrunners and loggers and, with a deep sea captain named Vosper, took off for the log dump.

163

With a donkey engine bolted to the forecastle head and another one aft on the main deck, just forward of the forward hatch, the *Malahat* fought its way up the coast. With auxiliary motors straining in heavy seas and all canvas up, it was a hair-raising journey. On one bad tack the wind blew the sails to ribbons; the jibs were flat in the water and twenty-foot high waves mounted the decks in mighty thrusts. Never in the Queen Charlottes before, Captain Vosper was soon lost in fog and heavy seas but he finally identified the area as very close to where they wanted to be. They anchored for the night and a tremendous wind and storm came up, blowing the ship stern-first half a mile up a river with branches pushing over from both sides. As luck would have it, the tide took them out again without the ship ever striking a snag.

Without knowing that he was creating the first log barge, Gibson had kept his crew busy tearing out 'tween decks and enlarging the hatch. The enlarging meant the removal of a mast and led to the mutiny of the captain and the former rum-runners. The captain did not appreciate Gibson cutting the mast down with a saw and the ropes with an axe but the logger won the argument, "because I was bigger than he was." Another nasty experience came when three huge logs stowed athwartships burst through a bulwark, taking out two of the ship's ribs almost to the waterline. Through a combination of ingenuity and luck, Gibson managed to ride out another storm that threatened to take them to Alaska instead of Port Alice, but they managed to deliver the cargo. There was enough money to pay the crew, including the mutineers, who decided to return to work since there was no other way to get south again, and a tidy profit for the Gibson brothers. The venture launched them into the log barging business. After that they always cleared at least $5,000 monthly, and on the strength of this success they bought three other old sailing ships, the *Forest Pride* and the *Kruse* from Seattle and the *Tolmie*, sister ship to the *Malahat*, in Victoria.

The Gibson brothers continued to prosper in other endeavors; at various times they have owned a fish-packing plant and fleet, a Vancouver radio station, a whaling station at Coal Harbor and a number of mining properties. Logging remained their main interest, however.

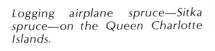

Logging airplane spruce—Sitka spruce—on the Queen Charlotte Islands.

Tahsis Mill as it looked in 1947 when the Gibson Brothers were in command. Company later sold to East Asiatic Company of Canada.

Nootka Cedar Company mill at Tahsis.

Between 1915 and 1938 small loggers worked A-frames in the Nootka Sound area close to Chief Maquinna's winter village, where Captain James Cook started it all back in 1778. But it was not until the Gibsons built a mill there in 1945 that the lumber industry of that area received its present impetus. A partnership between W.F. Gibson & Sons Ltd. with the East Asiatic Company Ltd. resulted in the formation of the Tahsis Company Ltd. East Asiatic bought out the Gibsons in 1952 and rapidly increased operations on its Tree Farm Licence which ranges from Zeballos in the north to south and east of Gold River, fifty miles away. Logging operations are located at Gold River, Zeballos and Sandpoint. Tahsis joined with Canadian International Paper Company in 1967 to build a pulp mill at Gold River at a cost of more than $60 million. Tahsis operates forty-five acres of seed orchard as part of a program that has established it as a leader among British Columbia forest companies in application of scientific forestry. At Gold River the company has a greenhouse for the growth of special stock, the only such greenhouse operated by a private forestry company in British Columbia. The company operates two sawmills now, the other being the Nootka Cedar Mill completed in 1970. About 1,600 people work for the firm.

165

Hammond Cedar Company's head rig, circular saws, 1926. This mill on the Fraser River traces its origin back to 1909 when it was known as the Port Hammond Sawmill. On May 31, 1946, it became part of British Columbia Forest Products.

12.
The Giants And The Gyppos

Many of today's Giants were yesterday's Gyppos, or independents.

Among the largest of these is the CANFOR group of companies, Canadian Forest Products Limited, and its affiliates, one hundred per cent privately owned by Canadians. The large, fully integrated forest industry complex, with woodland operations and manufacturing centres across Canada, employs a workforce of about 4,800 people.

Wood harvested by CANFOR is converted into lumber, plywood, shingles and shakes. Pulp chips are produced as a byproduct for the company's bleached sulphate mill at Port Mellon. The annual sales volume of lumber handled by CANFOR's products marketing division is approximately 500 million board feet, equivalent to the lumber required to build more than 50,000 typical single-family homes. CANFOR cedar sales group markets over 450,000 squares of shingles and shakes a year, enough to roof 18,000 average homes. Annual production of plywood and hardboard is equivalent to a stack of four foot by eight foot panels more than fifty miles high. CANFOR building materials division markets products in twenty-nine communities in Canada; it is also sales agent for plywood manufactured by two independent mills and a wholesale distributor of import and allied product lines.

The history of Canadian Forest Products Ltd. has been one of integration, starting with the establishment of a small veneer factory in New Westminster in 1938. The Englewood (a combination of the names of two early logging firms: Wood & English) Logging Division is a major source of wood for CANFOR coastal manufacturing plants. It is located primarily in the watershed of the Nimpkish River on northern Vancouver Island. Four residential communities are located there: Woss Camp, the central and largest, has a modern school and an airstrip;

Steam donkey raising a spar tree in Woss Camp area around 1953. Note the woodpile alongside.

167

Nimpkish, a railroad maintenance centre; Vernon Camp and Beaver Cove, the tidewater terminus of the railroad. A mobile camp is located at Atluck Lake. A truck-feeder system for hauling logs to the railway combines the flexibility of the truck logging with the economy of the railroad for long-distance transportation.

Claude Hunter, operator of giant sized speeder which transported Nimpkish River workers to various camps now run by CANFOR.

Big Douglas fir cut in Vernon Camp area of Canadian Forest Products. Bud Frost poses for camera.

Interior of sawmill of Woods & English at Englewood in 1926. Name Englewood was combination of these two names.

Running a base line through timber in Woss area around 1956. Loggers and cruisers worked in the wintertime too.

CANFOR's Eburne Sawmills on the north arm of the Fraser River employs about 600 persons in three sawmills, two planer mills, eleven dry kilns, barge and scow facilities. Booms of logs are towed to the mill with hemlock the chief species processed there.

Huntting-Merritt shingle division and Stave Lake cedar division are centred at Dewdney with a combined work force of about three hundred. Huntting-Merritt has sixteen shingle machines; Stave has twelve. The former became part of CANFOR in 1948, Stave Lake in 1943. Huntting-Merritt Mill was built on the present site in 1914 and rebuilt after a fire in 1920. The original Stave Lake mill was at Ruskin. The present mill was built in 1959 on the site of a smaller mill which was built in 1939 and destroyed later by fire.

CANFOR also has a division at Chetwynd, 195 miles northeast of Prince George. The company maintains up to 200 miles of logging roads in the area with timber coming mostly from contractors who truck it in from twenty to seventy-five miles away.

Canada's motto "A Mari Usque Ad Mare", From Sea To Sea, could equally apply to another of the forest giants' competitors, Weldwood Of Canada, which operates in all ten Provinces from the Pacific to the Atlantic. Weldwood's investment in plant, property and equipment amounts to more than $30 million and its assets exceed $145 million. It has plywood and lumber manufacturing facilities as well as logging operations in both Western and Eastern Canada. There are eighteen wood converting facilities: five plywood plants, five sawmills and two planer mills in British Columbia. The company is the largest single producer of both softwood and hardwood plywood. In 1973 alone it produced enough to encircle the world at the equator with a three-eighth inch, four foot wide path. It ranks fifth in Canada and eleventh in North America.

Incorporated in British Columbia in March, 1964, Weldwood is owner of a pulp mill in Quesnel with Daishowa-Marubeni; it took over the operations of Western Plywood Co. Ltd., Hay and Co. Ltd. and Westwood-Westply Ltd., Weldwood purchased Canadian Colleries Resources, a major forest products company that started as a coal mining firm on Vancouver Island, entering the forest industry only in 1957. The company employs about 4,400 people, most of whom work in its logging and manufacturing operations in British Columbia.

The history of British Columbia Forest Products Limited as a company dates back only to 1946. However, it was formed by the merger of several well-established and flourishing businesses which dated back to almost the turn of the century. Canadian industrialist E.P. Taylor and his associates became interested in the West Coast lumbering business in 1946 and incorporated a private company known as Vancouver Cedar & Spruce Limited. This company acquired Sitka Spruce Lumber Company which was operating a spruce mill in the False Creek area of Vancouver. This mill had no timber stands and was dependent on the open log market for wood. In May of 1946, Vancouver Cedar & Spruce Limited changed its name to British Columbia Forest Products Limited and became a public company. It then acquired Hammond Cedar Company, Cameron Lumber Company Limited, Victoria; and Hemmingsen-Cameron Company Limited.

British Columbia Forest Products also purchased two American-promoted firms: Malahat Logging Company and San Juan Lumber Company, then in July, 1946, acquired the assets of the Oscar Niemi

Building a bridge across Davie River in Nimpkish area 1954.

Clearing track for laying of rails at Englewood in 1926. Canadian Forest Products still runs a railroad "show" at Englewood.

Logging in Surrey, B.C. around 1895. Note the "greaser" has his pail of whale or crude oil to keep the logs slippery for the horses to pull that big log along the skidroad.

169

Pretty as a painting, and pretty well painted too! Kathy Vetleson, 19, daubs logs with various colors to indicate whose they are and where in the area they came from and under which form of tenure, Tree Forest Licence, etc. She had been working for CANFOR for about a year.

CANFOR superintendent Jack Vetleson watches mobile steel spar loading big log on truck at Woss Camp area. Also seen are Nels Olson (left) and Bill Vetleson. Grapple operator is Norm Ellis.

Company Limited, chiefly timberlands in the Britain River area. Oscar Niemi had logged there during the 1940s and BCFP followed his example by operating the Britain River camp complete with its own store, school and recreation facilities until closure in 1957. Blackstock Logging Company sold its chief assets to BCFP while Jervis Inlet Timber Company was bought out in December, 1948. That company was one of the oldest logging shows in Jervis Inlet.

BCFP employs a staff of professional foresters and engineers to improve the stock and increase yield of its timber holdings. Planting immediately after logging is followed and in five years about 11,000,000 selected seedlings have been planted on 33,000 acres of forest land. The company is part owner of a water bomber fleet and owns Swiftsure Towing Company Ltd. to transport the major portion of its logs in booms and self-loading, self-dumping barges. It operates four sawmills and a studmill, as well as two plywood plants, a veneer plant, two kraft pulp mills and a newsprint mill. Third largest lumber producer in Canada, BCFP employs 5,300 people.

Crown Zellerbach Canada Limited employs about 5,900 people across Canada. Virtually all its manufacturing plants are in British Columbia. It has extensive logging operations—company and contractor—on Vancouver Island, Queen Charlotte Islands, the British Columbia Mainland and in the Interior; one pulp and paper mill at Campbell River; a lumber mill and plywood complex in Coquitlam; lumber mills at Richmond, Campbell River, Kelowna, Lumby, Armstrong; plywood manufacturing plants at Kelowna and Armstrong; a bin and pallet operation at Kelowna; wood products laboratory and major paper products converting plant in Richmond and corrugated container manufacturing plant in Kelowna and plastic packaging plants in Richmond and Winnipeg. C-Z is credited with pioneering the use of wood chips and sawdust in British Columbia pulp manufacturing and in the early 1950s the company built, at Campbell River, the first newsprint mill to be constructed in the Province in thirty-five years.

Crown Zellerbach began its Canadian operations in 1914 with the acquisition of a small pulping operation at Ocean Falls, 325 miles north of Vancouver. The Provincial Government of that time had encouraged Crown Willamette Company of Oregon and Washington to move in. Pacific Mills Limited was formed to take over the properties of the defunct Ocean Falls Company. Crown Zellerbach managed the Ocean Falls mill for fifty-eight years until 1972 when an announcement was made that it would be phased out by early 1973 due to its uneconomic operation. The mill and townsite were sold to the Provincial Government in March, 1973 and the Crown-operated firm then claimed to have made a substantial profit.

CZ operates Fraser Mills, the historic McLaren mill at Millside in Coquitlam, British Columbia, which began operations in the late 19th century. In 1965 the pioneer Okanagan forest products firm of S.M. Simpson Limited joined Crown Zellerbach Canada's organization, while in 1969 the company acquired Armstrong Saw Mills Ltd., which has operations at Armstrong, Enderby, Falkland and supporting timber reserves. A new plant constructed at River Road, Richmond, at the end of 1974 replaces the Burnaby Seaforth plant destroyed by fire earlier that year.

Cathels & Sorenson Logging Company fell this big tree back in 1926. W.F. Cathels and C.S. Sorenson were bought out in 1933 by Matt Hemmingsen who formed Hemmingsen-Cameron, a firm that was later purchased by B.C. Forest Products Ltd.

A view of Ocean Falls as it looked in December, 1941. Looking up "A" street from the dock. Author worked here nine years later when it was said that Ocean Falls was named that because: "The sky opens up and the Ocean Falls," indicating that precipitation was above normal for rest of B.C.

Crown Zellerbach Canada is owned by CZ International with the exception of about ten per cent held by Canadians.

Alaska Pine and Cellulose Co. was formed in 1939 by Leon and Walter Koerner, recent immigrants to Canada from Czechoslovakia. The company set out to make Western hemlock saleable and succeeded by renaming it Alaska white pine. Koerner interests expanded rapidly and merged in 1951 with British Columbia Pulp and Paper Company and became Alaska Pine and Cellulose Ltd. In 1954 eighty per cent of the company's stock was bought by Rayonier Incorporated of New York. The most recent climax in the company's history occurred in 1968 when the giant International Telephone and Telegraph Corporation acquired control of Rayonier Incorporated of New York. Rayonier has logging operations at Jordan River (Canadian Puget Sound, southern Vancouver Island); Sewell Inlet (Queen Charlottes); Port McNeill (Pioneer Timber Company, northeastern Vancouver Island); Holberg, Mahatta River and Jeune Landing (northern Vancouver Island) and contractor logging operations at Gardner Canal and Loughborough Inlet on the Coast Mainland, Winter Harbor on northern Vancouver Island, Spuzzum Creek in the Fraser Valley and in the Queen Charlottes. Rayonier has lumber mills in New Westminster, Marpole and Silvertree, all on the North Arm of the Fraser River. It has a silvichemicals plant in Marpole, a district in south Vancouver, which produces—from hemlock bark—oilwell drilling mud dispersant, fertilizer and water clarifier. It has a pulp mill at Port Alice and one at Woodfibre. Western Forest Industries, an affiliated company, operates lumber and shingle mills at Honeymoon Bay near Lake Cowichan and logging at Gordon River.

Seaboard is the exclusive export sales organization for a number of British Columbia sawmills and plywood plants, producing softwood

Topping the spar tree. After yelling Timberrr, the highrigger braces himself for the shock that occurs as giant tree waves back and forth. Spar trees are seldom used anymore as logging companies have mobile steel spars which yard timber in formerly inaccessible areas.

lumber, softwood plywood, decorative plywood, hardboard, shingles and shakes. The shareholding mills operate thirty-four sawmills, eleven plywood mills, five shingle and shake mills and a hardboard plant. The success achieved by Seaboard is mainly due to economies resulting from large volume and many different wood products, the output of the above-mentioned diverse organizations. Since its inception in 1935, Seaboard has become one of the world's largest exporters of wood products. More than 18,000 people are directly employed by the Seaboard mills in their logging camps, plants and organizations. Seaboard Shipping Company Limited was established in 1936 to transport the wood products sold by Seaboard Lumber sales from British Columbia to

customers overseas. A Seaboard charter vessel leaves British Columbia approximately every five days on a year-round basis.

Canadian Cellulose Company Limited was incorporated in 1964 under the name of Skeena Kraft Limited and began construction of a kraft mill in Prince Rupert. A predecessor, Columbia Cellulose Company Limited, was incorporated by Celanese Corporation of New York in 1946. In 1959 Concel acquired Celgar Limited which operated sawmills in the Arrow Lakes region and which in 1960 constructed a new saw-

During World War II many women worked in pulp and papermills. Here a woman grades paper.

Break in the paper on number one machine at Pacific Mills, Ocean Falls, circa 1944.

172

Doctor Walter Koerner with the late Governor General Vincent Massey and other dignitaries outside Alaska White Pine, the company he formed with his brothers Leon and Otto in 1939. By proving that Western hemlock was a superior wood, they expanded and in 1951 merged with B.C. Pulp & Paper Company to form Alaska Pine & Cellulose. Rayonier Inc. bought 80 per cent of firm in 1954.

Mobile log loader in operation at Canadian Puget Sound operation at Jordan River on Vancouver Island. CPS is a firm controlled by Rayonier.

mill and pulp mill at Castlegar. Celgar was merged into Skeena Kraft in 1970 and on June 29, 1973, the British Columbia Government acquired seventy-nine per cent of the Canadian Cellulose stock and Canadian Cellulose acquired all the assets of Colcel. In 1959 Colcel became a public company affiliated with the Celanese Corporation whose operations in Canada, the United States and Mexico are major consumers of sulphite pulp. Late in 1969 Canadian Cellulose acquired the Pohle Lumber Mill in Terrace. Canadian Cellulose's organization stretches from British Columbia's southern interior to its northern coast and utilizes the skills of approximately 3,000 people.

Weyerhaeuser Canada Limited is an integrated forest products company with operations in the southern interior of British Columbia. The company employs about 2,000 people in its Canadian operations which include a bleached kraft pulp mill in Kamloops, sawmills at Merritt, Kamloops, Lumby and Vavenby. The British Columbia sawmills produce about 310 million board feet of softwood, kiln-dried dimension lumber annually.

Eurocan Pulp & Paper Co. Ltd. was incorporated in British Columbia in May, 1965, and is jointly owned by three Finnish pulp and paper companies. Eurocan's manufacturing facilities consist of a woodmill and pulp and paper mill located in Kitimat, 400 miles north of Vancouver. The company carries on logging operations in its coastal Tree Farm Licence and has an Interior logging division at Burns Lake.

In just a little over a decade Northwood Mills Ltd. has become the second largest marketer of lumber in Canada. A wholly-owned subsidiary of Noranda, through its own subsidiary, Northwood Properties Ltd., it operates four sawmills in British Columbia: at Okanagan Falls, Penticton and Princeton. Northwood also operates a door and molding manufacturing plant and cut-up and box plant as well as lumber and building sales and distribution facilities in British Columbia, Alberta, Manitoba, Ontario and Quebec. Northwood Mills holds a fifty per cent

More and more women are being hired in a variety of jobs in the forest industry including tree-planting, slash evaluation and scaling. This pretty lumberjill works for Rayonier.

interest in Northwood Pulp and Timber which manufactures kraft pulp. Four thousand people are employed in the company which set a trend in reforestation programs by introducing women into planting operations near McGregor, British Columbia. Since then other forestry operations have hired women for this important work.

Loading big logs onto ship in Vancouver harbor.

Loading plywood in Vancouver Harbor. B.C.'s integrated forest industry firms combine efficiency with utilization of increasing amount of resource that was formerly left to waste.

Loading packaged lumber at Vancouver harbor.

Tom Behan operates a shingle machine.

The giants of the forest include Canadian Forest Products (CANFOR), Weldwood, Rayonier, British Columbia Forest Products, Crown Zellerbach, MacMillan Bloedel, Weyerhaeuser, Northwood, Eurocan, Canadian Cellulose, Seaboard and Tahsis.

174

Looking up to the sky through an umbrella of trees.

Horses and men take a short break for the photographer in this wintertime scene somewhere in British Columbia at the turn of the century.

There is another giant forest firm which doesn't make a direct profit, nor does it sell anything but goodwill. The Council of Forest Industries represents and acts on behalf of companies in all areas of common interest except industrial relations and selling. COFI members and affiliated members produce ninety per cent of the total product value of the British Columbia forest industry. It serves its members in the areas of accident control, forestry and logging, government and public relations, log security, research and development, statistics and transporation. But the most important COFI function is wood product promotion. Member committees and staff work to create an acceptance and demand for the lumber, plywood, shingles and shakes produced by member companies. COFI is administered by a president, four vice-presidents and a staff of more than 130 persons under the guidance of a board of directors and senior operating committees drawn from segments of the membership.

175

This may have been the way it was with the very early camps in B.C. The bunkhouse was the same place where men ate, slept and had their leisure hours. Smoke escaped past the drying clothing through a hole in the roof. Home was never like this!

13.
United They Stand
The International Woodworkers of America — another forest giant.

Unionization of the forest industry in British Columbia is a story of adventure, intrigue and violence. A combination of force, coercion and propaganda were used to keep loggers from forming unions; but repressive as those measures were, day to day existence in the early camps was enough to keep some loggers trying for a better deal. At the turn of the century, loggers and millworkers who had managed to survive inhuman toil found their rewards on city skidroads. With broken backs and burned out guts, many finished up in flop houses and charity hostels. Early attempts to unionize loggers were difficult because the camps almost always had three crews: one coming in, one working and one leaving. A man on the move was a hard man to talk to about anything.

Conditions under which these drifting workmen lived were similar in many ways to those in the earlier Industrial Revolution in Europe. Bunkhouses were filthy and infested with bed bugs and lice. Bad food was served on battered enamel plates which housed all manner of bacteria. Clothes were dried in the crowded discomfort of the bunkhouse which was badly lit and poorly ventilated. Washrooms were unknown. Men found their own latrines in the bush and lined up for the use of outside wash basins. Each man packed his own blankets from camp to camp and a portion of his day's earnings was deducted for the use of a rotten mattress and unappetizing fare on the cookshack table. Early loggers didn't even have mattresses on their tiered bunks; some of the bunks were stacked four high. Charlie Hemstrom of Honeymoon Bay, Vancouver Island, came from Sweden in 1906 to work as a greaser on the skidroads. Living conditions were deplorable, he admitted, "but we weren't used to much anyway." Many early camps kept pigs which

This old camp was run by Channel Logging Company and burned down in May, 1923.

177

became table fare after they had been fattened up on bracken and table scraps. Hemstrom recalled going into the pig pen once to get some clean straw to sleep on. "They nearly canned me for that, for taking the straw," he said. "You were supposed to sleep on tree boughs or nothing."

Owen Brown said logging operators established their own working conditions. A former International Woodworkers of America Local president, Brown said the loggers had to turn out to work under any and all conditions. Production or "highball" was the order of the day and safety practices were unknown. Workers were a dime a dozen and if one was killed during working hours (sunrise to sunset and six or seven days a week), he was quickly replaced by another more active body. Burial procedures took place when it became convenient. Some bodies lay in coastal camps for weeks until a ship came by and they could be taken out. Others, like "Old Tompkins" at Campbell River who was interred by a half dozen of his mates rousted out of the beer parlor by the local minister, were buried in simple graves. A whiskey bottle, like the one that did him in, was Old Tompkins' memorial and placed in the the grave along with the body. Scant attention was paid to most of these remembrance services. The logger's belongings may have consisted of a cheap suitcase, two suits of dirty underwear, two bug-ridden blankets, a watch that didn't work and a thumb-worn photograph of a mother or sweetheart in a foreign country.

Owen Brown, describing typical working conditions said a hooktender on a highball operation would be standing three or four hundred feet out of the sight of the chokerman. "He would see you dive in the bush there, then estimate how long it would take you to set the choker," he said. "Then he'd give the go-ahead and never wait to see if you were clear. This is how so many men got killed in the early days of logging."

Early float camp. Loggers were so isolated in a setting like this that they had to wait until a boat came to take them off even if they quit or were fired.

The first shift at the Englewood camp of Woods & English in 1926. The men were all white.

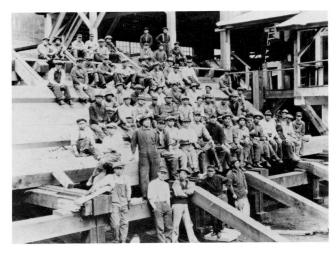

The second shift at the Englewood camp of Woods & English in 1926. The men were all Oriental.

178

Former IWA president of Duncan local, Weldon Jubenville, said the companies did not even supply the men with tools. "We had to supply our own wedges, saws and axes," he said. There was no paid transportation to the job, no health and welfare, no statutory holidays, no seniority and no vacations with pay. "You didn't have any security," Jubenville said. "Management could fire you any time they wanted to and for any reason. You had no recourse." No grievance procedures.

But the quitting was easy. In those days it was the logger's only weapon, albeit a puny one. When the markets were good, jobs were plentiful so a faller or bucker fired here today, went there tomorrow. You just went to the office and asked for your time and it was made out immediately, one oldtimer said. "No income tax deductions, no deductions for medical plan, no group insurance, no unemployment insurance. Of course, there was your store bill, if the camp was big enough to sport such a convenience. And your room and board." There was no such thing as leave of absence, for whatever reason. Again, quitting was the only answer. But if you were a good logger and the boss liked you, you might get a slip with your pay that said: "Return anytime."

The camp of International Timber Company at Campbell River as it looked in 1926.

A lot of men were fired for union activity, which was forbidden. Others got the boot simply because the superintendent didn't like their faces. One big super at Great Central Lake in the bad years was feared because he was not only tough but he literally held the loggers' jobs in the palm of his hand. "You had to stay on the run around him all the time," says a logger who worked there. "He'd fire you as soon as look at you then put somebody in your place who'd crossed his palm with a couple of bucks." The super got his just desserts one day when a big Swede who had been hired the previous day sauntered rather than ran past him to the crummy. The super jerked his thumb at him and told him he was fired. It was in the days when a logger made his own lunch and so the Swede walked up and slammed his lunch bucket against the super's head. "You could at least of fired me before I made my lunch!" he yelled.

During one slump, when men were more plentiful than jobs, retired logger Elton Anderson went job hunting at a camp called O'Malley's on the Cowichan River. Two blocks on a cable were employed to transport loggers across to the camp on Riverbottom Road. The day Anderson got there the blocks were both on the other side. "I was so desperate for a job," he said, "I went hand over hand across the river on the cable. My hands cramped like hell in the middle but I took one look at that deep water and I got my strength back right away." Safely on the other side, he walked a half mile to the camp and sought out the "push." "How'd you get here?" the man wanted to know. Figuring to cover himself with glory and land a well-earned job, Anderson explained his fortitude and initiative. "Well," the bush boss said, "you're in luck. Going back you'll be able to use the block."

In those days, particularly in the Depression when jobs were scarce in the woods and mill, anyone who even talked union was sent down the road whistling to himself. Loggers with determination still lectured on

179

Early crummies like this one were used to transport loggers to the job sites. They got to the camp on their own, however, and had to supply their own tools and bed-rolls.

Only four men to a room—and a radio too! Things were looking up at Industrial Timber Mills Camp 6 during 1934. Left to right were Harry Hobson, Tom Fraser, Harold Pleger and Larry Rowland.

the skidroad in Vancouver, however, hoping to gain support for their cause. Many people, including some loggers, jeered at these orators with their hand-painted placards and soapbox antics. The speakers were often deeply committed to socialist-communist ideals, and were unable to imagine achieving better working conditions without adhering to those aspirations.

Not all loggers could accept both objectives in one package, and some managements used this uncertainty to their advantage, spreading the word that unionism meant "Red" domination of the province's primary industry. Eventually the time came when logging unions favoring Communism and those merely wanting a better deal without any political affiliation came to a major disagreement. The "October Revolution" took place in that month in 1948 when a group of dissidents from the International Woodworkers of America union broke away to form the Woodworkers' Industrial Union of Canada. The next year was crowded with confrontations as the two segments battled for control of the membership. The IWA finally triumphed by virtue of their well organized financial and pressure tactics. However, the IWA must acknowledge its debt to the Lumber Workers' Industrial Union, the earlier B.C. Loggers' Union and particularly the Industrial Workers of the World, the IWW, or "Wobblies" as they were best known.

A Wobbly song, "The Lumberjack's Prayer", expresses the mood of the period:

> I pray dear Lord, for Jesus' sake,
> Give us this day a T-bone steak.
> Hallowed be Thy name.
> But don't forget to send the same.
>
> O hear my humble cry, O Lord.
> And send me down some decent board.
> Brown gravy and some German fried,
> With sliced tomatoes on the side.

O hear me Lord: remove those "dogs",
Those sausages of powdered logs.
The bullbeef hash and bearded sprouts.
Take them to Hell or thereabouts.

With alum bread and pressed beef butts,
Dear Lord they've damn near ruined my guts.
Their white-washed milk and oleorine,
I wish to Christ I'd never seen.

There was very little humor in the songs striking workers sang to taunt police during the Blubber Bay, Texada Island, strike of 1938-39. Grant MacNeil, then a Member of Parliament, wrote in the *Western Canadian Lumber Worker*, a trade publication, that the dispute at Pacific Lime Company was "against the most brutal police and company tyranny in British Columbia."

An inside view of a typical British Columbia bunkhouse in the Dirty Thirties. Obviously the bullcook has gone on strike. Notice the pinup girls at the back on the left.

The "tyranny" began in July, 1937, when the company refused to negotiate with employees over grievances, many of them involving job hazards. The company manager's position was that the IWA—which had replaced the earlier Lumber and Sawmill Workers Union—was Communist-led. The Vancouver *Sun* reported that the strike was really a fight between the then-rival American Federation of Labor and the Congress of Industrial Organizations. (The AFL and CIO have since affiliated.) The situation continued to deteriorate over a period of two years with Provincial Police, forerunners of the RCMP, pulling the taunting pickets off the line and jailing them, but up until a strike was called on June 2, 1938, there was no violence. Then, MacNeil wrote, "terrorist tactics were employed by company officials." Chinese workers were evicted from their quarters "under threats of clubs and tear

181

gas" and white workers were forced out of company-owned homes and in many instances their personal belongings disappeared," MacNeil said.

Colin Cameron, Member of the Legislative Assembly of British Columbia, also went to Texada, where he was held in police custody when he protested on behalf of the Chinese. MacNeil was not allowed to move from place to place in the area without a police escort. Then Bob Gardiner, vice-president of Local 163, was arrested early one morning, taken from his house, and severely beaten at the temporary police headquarters on the island. He was hospitalized in Powell River but he later died as a result of his injuries after serving part of a four-month jail sentence at Oakalla Prison. The union brought the police constable responsible for the beating to trial and he was sentenced to six months in jail. Twenty-seven other police and strike breakers were brought to trial by the IWA but all were acquitted. Fifteen strikers were charged with rioting and unlawful assembly and given a total of forty-nine months in Oakalla. Colin Cameron returned to the Legislature in Victoria to assail Attorney General Gordon Wismer of the Liberal Government for "illegal brutality of police tactics". MacNeil told the story of the strike in the next session of the House of Commons in Ottawa and moved an amendment to the Criminal Code which would prevent the use of the unlawful assembly section to break strikes. The section still stands.

During this period, men all over British Columbia were being sent to jail for activities also termed "unlawful assembly" and for "trespassing" on company property. But they persisted, ignoring blacklisting, harrassment and other indignities. Organizers who couldn't get jobs because of the blacklisting assumed false names, were re-hired and continued to spread the union word. Some companies fought back, buying radio time to broadcast anti-union messages and dropping propaganda leaflets by plane. The broadcasts and the leaflets warned of the danger of a "Red" takeover of the province's number one industry. They imported workers from the Prairies to take over jobs of men ousted for union activities.

Some incidents were amusing, at least in retrospect. At one big camp in the Alberni Valley area, police and company men guarded the entrance to keep out an "invasion" by union agitators. The invaders arrived and after a short confrontation with the guards, went quietly on their way. Meanwhile, the real organizers had snuck in by another route and were signing up members in the bunkhouses.

One enterprising camp superintendent decided to carry on his own war against the union men. When some workers tried to get back to Great Central Lake to confront the "scabs" who had taken their jobs over, the super jumped into his big powerful Ford twin-engine speedboat and tried to dampen the hopes of the logger pickets. The union men were in rowboats which threatened to capsize as the big powerboat circled them. On one trip around, bobbing in his own wake, the super failed to notice a big deadhead in the water. He hit it and with boat stove in and no offers of aid, he silently cursed his watery reward while the loggers continued peacefully up to the lakehead.

Cecil Clark, Deputy Chief of the Provincial Police at that time, said that it must be remembered that there were very different attitudes by

Speeder "crummy" transporting crew at Woss Camp in 1954.

182

police, companies—and the public, too—towards unions in those days. "Those were really the bad old days," Clark commented. He was not apologizing for the behavior of some police, like the special constable on Texada and others there, but explaining that circumstances were totally different then.

Wages continued to be low in the mills during the Thirties—they were, in fact, cut in some years—and labor organizing continued at a brisk pace. The mills had the benefit of being centralized and near communities. It was different at the logging camps, most of which were hard to reach, where the distribution of union information was banned. The "union rag" *B.C. Lumber Worker* was forbidden and anyone caught reading it was liable for instant dismissal.

Nonetheless, unionists found that on-the-site organizing was the most effective and began taking their soapboxes into the woods to harangue workers during lunchtime and after work. Company officials and the co-operative Provincial Police endeavored to keep union men away from the camps, but they got in anyway. In clearings in the bush, away from the ears of the camp boss, loggers were told by organizers that they were second class citizens whose only future lay on the city skidroads. "You don't get paid enough to live like humans," the organizers said. "You're treated like animals. You don't have any choice boys, you have to organize."

These woodland gatherings seemed to meet with more success than rallies held in halls in the city. When a logger came to town with a stake he felt more like hoisting a few in the Stanley Hotel pub than going to hear a talk on collective bargaining. And the realities of the harsh life in the bush tended to fade with each drink.

One breakthrough came when about two hundred loggers set up a strike camp of tents near their Campbell River job site where scab labor was employed. Victory didn't net them everything they wanted but they proved that the general public was on their side.

According to Myrtle Bergren in her excellent book on unionization of the logging industry, *Tough Timber*, the real foothold came at Lake Log Camp at Cowichan in 1934 when the Lumber Workers Industrial Union managed to negotiate a contract with that firm which had employed about three hundred men, most of them blacklisted militants. They were also good loggers and this was recognized by camp superintendent Neil MacDonald who only wanted to move logs, not face labor problems.

Problems between union, management and government will continue but the Bad Old Days are over. Loggers now can claim fare allowances, travel time, decent food, excellent wages, clean bunkhouses, recreational facilities, stabilized board rates, safety programs and most of the benefits enjoyed by workers in other fields.

"Oh, the railroad runs through the middle of the house," sang Vaughan Monroe many years ago. "And the trains were all on time. Here comes the five-o-nine." The Climax No. 3 is coming through the bunkhouses at Camp 5, west of Ladysmith. "All aboard!"

Clean bunkhouses, good food, high pay, a pride in the job are all part of the new way of life for the logger.

The final verse of the Lumberjack's Prayer sums up their new situation:

> O hear me Lord, I'm praying still.
> But if you don't, our Union will
> Put pork chops on the bill of fare
> And starve no workers anywhere.

183

Tugboat fleet lined up in a rare get together on the Fraser River. August 8, 1928.

184

14.
Tugging Along
Logging down the Ocean Highway.

If you were to scale a straight line along the Forty Ninth Parallel to the Sixtieth Parallel of latitude you would find it measures about 950 miles. But if you were to follow a road along that rugged British Columbia coast, inching through each long inlet and sound, you would cover about 12,000 miles. The road would cut through a thousand fingers of the sea and intervening barriers of granite. Luckily for the loggers, who needed a good highway to get their product from its increasingly inaccessible source to the market, the route was already there: The Ocean. All that was required was some means of moving the logs on that highway; it seems fitting that the pioneer steamer on the Pacific Coast should also have the honor of being one of the earliest tugboats of any consequence.

The famous Hudson's Bay Company Beaver, seen here hauling cattle and other supplies, was British Columbia's first log towing boat.

The *Beaver*, the Hudson's Bay Company vessel that had already distinguished herself as a passenger and trading ship, was refitted as a towboat in 1874.

185

While the steam tug *Diana*, purchased in San Francisco by Captain Edward Stamp and used in 1862 to tow sailing vessels in and out of Port Alberni as well as for coastal trips to Victoria, may also have towed some logs, the *Beaver* is generally credited with being the first to have been used specifically for that pupose. By the standards of the day she was little less than a marvel, her 100-foot hull was pushed by two side-lever engines to develop seventy-five horsepower—although some old-timers believe she was capable of up to 200 horsepower. *Beaver's* boilers were fired by wood billets and bark and required the services of a ten-man chopping crew who travelled with her wherever she went. After being burned, sunk, and raised again, the *Beaver* operated in good order for British Columbia Towing and Transportation Company as a towboat until 1888 when she was once more licensed for transporting passengers. But she continued her logging duties, taking men and supplies to the camps up the coast from Vancouver until she was wrecked at Prospect Point on July 26, 1888. In her last days she was owned by Hastings Sawmills which had operations in Shoal Bay on Thurlow Island.

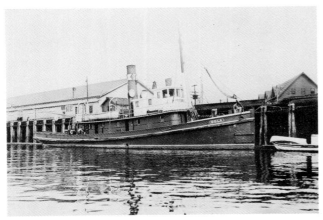

Old log towing steam tug Dola.

Cloe towing logs for Brooks, Scanlon & O,Brian at Stillwater, 1926.

Other boats began to be built or converted for log towing purposes. Early Vancouver entrepreneur Jerry Rogers, who cleared the original site for the Hastings Mill at the foot of what is now Dunlevy Street in Vancouver, built the tugboat *Maggie* in 1873 on a platform in front of the Granville Hotel. She was a wooden boat, seventy-two feet long, with a twenty horsepower engine. She worked for the Hastings Mill for about ten years.

A fifty-four foot tug called the *Union* was built about 1874; her engine was originally designed to be in a threshing machine and had many complicated gears and belts to drive a set of paddles. Her peculiar machinery and method of operation led her detractors to nickname her the "Sudden Jerk" after the engineer once was forced to throw a sack of potatoes into the gears to stop the boat.

In old reports, the *Iris* is mentioned as arriving from Westminster in July, 1884, with a load of lumber from De Beck's Mill, and in the same year the original *Belle* of the Hastings Mill is mentioned. Also, the tug *Lillie* took lumber to Port Moody from the Royal City Planing Mills. In

1884 the *Mermaid* was built in Victoria and was operated on Burrard Inlet by R.M. Alexander. Another early tug was the *Etta White*, built at Freeport, Washington, by Captain George White. After running for a while on Puget Sound she was sold to the Moodyville Sawmill in 1875. She was a wood-burning screw boat with two-cylinder simple engines. When the Hastings Mill took over the Moodyville Company, *Etta White* went along.

Any attempt to name all the tugs used for log towing in British Columbia waters, even those used in the early days, would be unsuccessful, but a few of the valiant vessels deserve mention.

On June 4, 1889, the *Lorne*, built for James Dunsmuir to tow sailing ships to his coal mines, was launched in Victoria. She also towed many logs; her huge 1,100 horsepower triple-expansion engines built by Victoria's Vulcan Iron Works operated very efficiently. The boat was finally junked in August, 1937, but not until she had written herself into history. The *Lorne* was always a source of irritation to American tugboat owners. She nearly always beat them to the scene of rescues, in both Canadian and American water, because of her superior speed. Puget Sound Tugboat Company of Seattle was happy to buy her from coal baron Dunsmuir. She was later wrecked in the San Juan Islands. But that didn't end *Lorne's* career. She was raised and went on to work for Grand Trunk Railway towing Sitka spruce during World War I. She became Canadian again working in the Merchant Marine and in the spring of 1924 made headlines for herself and her owners, Johnson Walton and Company, by towing a raft with 4 million feet of logs from the Queen Charlottes to Swanson Bay.

Built in 1907, the *Ivanhoe* was one of the first tugs purchased when Kingcome Navigation was formed in 1910. She towed her share of logs until "retiring" in 1971 to become the floating home of Mr. and Mrs. Withey of Sylva Bay.

The 1200 horsepower St. Faith *was put into service by Kingcome Navigation in 1926 for towing Davis rafts from northern waters to Powell River. As the S.D. Brooks, and later, Haida Monarch, she was Kingcome's flag ship for many years.*

In 1890, Captains Ford, Trehune and Young built the *Brunette*, selling her to the Brunette Mills for log towing from Snug Cove on Howe Sound to the New Westminster mill. She became the property of the M.R. Cliff Towing Company in 1920 who bought her from the Smith Dollar Com-

187

Brunette, oldest working tugboat on the B.C. coast, doing her stuff at Powell River harbor.

Captain Vic Di Castri, skipper of the oldest tugboat on the British Columbia coast. A veteran himself, Di Castri lovingly handles the 85 year old Brunette at Powell River.

pany and is today the proud possession of Captain Vic Di Castri of Powell River. Di Castri, who celebrated his fiftieth anniversary working on tugs in 1975, said the *Brunette* is capable of eleven knots, can stop on a dime and can out-manoeuvre any steel hulled tug designed to perform the same sort of tasks. The old tug was handled by many legendary captains, including A.C. "Simmy" Simpson who was her master for more than twenty years from 1926 until after the Second World War. Captain Simpson said the tug was always lucky for him and everybody else who sailed aboard her. She was sunk only once. That happened around the turn of the century when a slightly tipsy captain tried to run up the inside of some pilings in the Fraser River. Rescuers found the captain snoring in his bunk just above the water line with a huge piling jutting into the shattered wheelhouse a few inches from his head. The *Brunette* weathered the crisis better than the besotted captain. She was refloated; he was fired.

By the early 1900s smoke belching tugs were seen everywhere in British Columbia waters towing rafts of logs. These rafts were "flat", as the name implies, and weather prone in all but sheltered areas or exceedingly calm seas. Logs transported in "bag" booms fared no better. The bag raft was also prey to wind and tide, being nothing more than a corral of chained logs to enclose the loose timbers.

Cruising down the river by raft, this one being the Omineca, *Dunning Hoff of Fort St. James aboard.*

But three Canadians were working to change the methods of log booming. Captain H.R. Robertson of St. Johns, New Brunswick, developed a raft in the late 1800s. Logs were enclosed in a cradle that was built on land. The logs were then bound with chains. This method was not very successful at first. Two rafts Captain Robertson built to transport pilings from Coos Bay, Oregon, to California in 1891 or 1892 broke up and were lost at sea. In 1895 another raft of his built at Stella, Washington, was partially destroyed near Golden Gate Bridge but sixty per cent reached its destination in San Francisco and sold at a good profit. Clearly, the system was not perfected so Robertson, supported by another Canadian, lumberman H.B. Hammond, built "the greatest raft of all time", a giant sixty-feet wide, 835 feet long which contained 11 million board feet. The Hammond Lumber Company's steamer *Francis H. Leggett* made the successful tow to San Francisco, carrying her own load of 1,600,000 feet of lumber as well.

188

Simon Benson of Oregon and two other Americans, John A. Festabend and O.J. Evenson, improved upon the Robertson raft in 1906. Theirs had a simple cradle with an improved centre locking device and improved towing gear. It was named for Benson, one of the principals in Benson Timber Co. of Oregon and was constructed by using a floating cradle, or form, in sections, which could be removed when it was completed.

Another Canadian now entered the log rafting business: G.G. "Bert" Davis, superintendent of British Canadian Lumber Company Vancouver Island logging camp. Davis had been losing three out of every five rafts and the company for whom he worked was about to go out of business so he devised a method of bundling logs together that required neither forming cradle nor chains. The Davis raft was made up of sawmill length logs rather than the tree length required by both Benson and Robertson style rafts. A first layer of logs called a "mat" was laced together with wire rope with "side sticks" holding the inside logs in place. Succeeding layers of logs, parbuckled or donkey-loaded onto the mat, were one or two logs less than the layer below. Well secured with wire rope, the floating woodpiles could be made up into easily towed rafts containing as much as 5 million board feet. For almost forty years the giant ocean-going cigar known as the Davis raft was the most practical way to transport logs from the Queen Charlottes and the west coast of Vancouver Island. (Island Tug's *Sea Lion* towed the first Davis raft in 1916.)

Old sailing ship hull converted to haul logs. The first such conversion of this type was done by J. Gordon Gibson who used the Malahat, a five-masted schooner to bring out timber from the Queen Charlottes. This is the Island Forester. Barges of this type had difficult loading and unloading problems.

Building the rafts was a specialized job. Breaking them up was too. Bob Sage of Victoria got into the boom breaking business in the 1920s. He and his two older brothers, George and Bert, broke up Davis rafts for Cathels and Sorenson and firms in Victoria, Squamish and other locations. It was hard, dangerous work and not many men took a liking to it. "A few guys would try it for a while then find out how tough it was and go and do something else," Bob Sage said. "What we did first was to check the raft to see which cables would come off the clamps easily. Some of them we had to take the bolts off with our heads practically under the water if the log had turned. Occasionally the bolts would rust on or would be so tight they couldn't be loosened by wrenches so the one inch or one and a quarter inch cable would have to be cut. We carried an axe and a sledge hammer and sometimes that cable would jump thirty, forty feet when she was cut."

A typical boom showing construction.

The Sage trio suffered only one accident in their partnership which lasted from 1923 to 1939 and that was when George (who died in 1974 at the age of ninety-five) had a log roll on his leg and break it. It was at Canadian Western Cooperage in Victoria and "that was a small boom," Sage said, "only about 30,000 feet in it." The Sage brothers knew big booms too. One Davis raft containing 1.5 million board feet floated out of Pacific Logging's booming ground in Nootka Sound to Port Moody where the brothers waited to pull it apart.

The pay was good but the boom-breakers knew lean times too. Bob Sage worked as a camp cook, cabinet maker, cab driver and pile driver operator for such companies as MacDonald & Murphy at Crofton, Canadian Puget Sound and Kissinger (later, Charter Logging). Sage, a heavy man, recalls other brawlers who made it big in the forest industry: Leo Sweeney (the unofficial booster for the city of Vancouver) and Gordon Gibson, "The Million Dollar Logger". All three came to-

189

Log rafts off Capilano River, North Vancouver.

Booming grounds at Brown's Bay, Vancouver Island. Logs left in the water for any length of time are subject to infestation by the toredo, a worm that can ruin the logs in a very short time.

Bundled logs awaiting spring run-off for journey to Hope. Logs are from Bond Logging on Fraser River near Sheep Creek.

Log rafts in Pitt River. Rafts in this simple form of construction were likely to be broken up in even moderate seas. Davis raft was much better for ocean-going purposes.

gether the day Gibson arrived in Victoria from Tahsis with a load of logs in the converted sailing ship *Malahat*. "Gibson was a hard man to work for because he was such a hard worker himself," Sage said. "He expected everybody to work at his pace." With Sweeney ("another hard man to work for") yelling at him from the wharf and Gibson yelling at him from the ship, it was all Sage could do to yell back at both of them and still get his boom breaking done.

Sage Brothers also worked for H.R. MacMillan at Mill Bay, booming cedar telephone poles for San Francisco and fir for Japan. Although he never had any serious swimming incidents, Bob Sage took many a dunking—or, as he puts it: "tipped ass over tea kettle many's the time."

Boommen remain the heroes of the log moving end of the lumbering business because without them it couldn't be done. It was an absolute prerequisite for this job to be nimble for they are fated to spend a good deal of their working day leaping from log to floating log, some of which tend to roll violently or sink. The principle job is sorting with the "pikepole", a long rod with a sharpened end with which boommen push and pull logs in the water. Much of this work has now been taken over by boom boats, bouncy little ducks which nip in and out among the logs, snorting and sorting. Because it is dangerous work, booming is serious business. But boommen have fun too. Maurice Thomas of Fraser Mills tells of the time he and his workmates pretended they had found a body in the Fraser River near the booming area. They propped up a dummy they had made in the boomshack and men from all over the mill came to peer in the window at it. "Somehow the radio got hold of the story that a body had been found in the river and the old townsite constable came down, and then the Provincials," Thomas said. "They really believed it. We all had a good laugh but we really got raked over the coals for that one."

Despite the improvements made through the years in rafts and towboats, weather is always a problem and delays are common—and expensive. Wood boring toredos infest the logs, tunnelling their way into the hearts of the wood in a short time, destroying or damaging large amounts before it can be utilized. A three-week round trip from the Queen Charlottes is common. Worming along, taking shelter in the coves on the way back, the tugboat men might be holed up for weeks waiting for a break in the weather.

Over a period of many years experiments have been made to improve log shipment methods. Old sailing ships were stripped to the hull and filled with forest bounty. They towed well but had little else to commend them. Then came an historic event: Island Tug & Barge(now Seaspan International) sent its powerful *Sudbury* and *Island Sovereign* on a 5,000 mile trip to Venezuela to tow four tankers in a line from there to drydock in Victoria. These old ships and others like them became log-carrying barges.

MacMillan Bloedel, through its wholly-owned subsidiary Kingcome Navigation, then began constructing self-loading, self-dumping log barges designed specifically for the job. *Haida Carrier*, heralded at the time as the largest of these barges in the world was launched at Yarrows Shipyard in Esquimalt on May 15, 1961. At 340 feet long with a sixty-four foot beam, she draws less than twenty feet fully loaded. She

"We'll take two over here, waiter!" Boomman at Lake Cowichan operation gets logs ready for the big move to the mill.

Crown Zellerbach's M.V. Hecate Crown was built to brave frequent storms and high winds in Queen Charlotte Sound where she tows self-loading and unloading barges capable of carrying 2.2 million board feet of logs per trip. The tug is 131 feet long and is all guts.

191

Another tug from the Kingcome fleet is the sleek Harmac Cedar.

Cheerful Nootka is Captain Willie George in the Tidal Wave.

Early style of boom boat in scenic setting on Howe Sound. These boom boats, or dozer boats, have taken away a lot of the work that formerly was done by boommen, although boommen are still very much a part of the logging scene.

Reg Embleton breaks up a log jam at Mac-Millan Bloedel's Menzies Bay dump.

Janet Crosley herds log bundle with dozer boat at MacMillan Bloedel's Cameron Division booming grounds.

192

can carry 1.5 million feet of logs loaded by means of two cranes mounted on pedestals on the hull. The logs simply slide off her broad back after special tanks in the hull are flooded to tilt the barge thirty-five degrees. She self-rights. MB's *Haida Carrier* and British Columbia Forest Products' *Forest Prince*, launched shortly afterward, symbolized the arrival of a new era of log transportation in British Columbia. Scheduled runs from the Charlottes to the log sorting grounds in Georgia Strait can now be made in three days instead of three weeks.

Members of the British Columbia Towboat Owner's Association supply tug services for almost any towing job and some of the Forest Giants have their own fleets. Crown Zellerbach inherited a fleet begun in 1911 under Canadian Western Lumber Company Ltd. In the summer of 1912, Canadian Tugboat Company Ltd. took delivery of these four coal-fired steam tugs with the Disneyish names of *Cheerful, Fearful, Joyful* and *Dreadful*. As might be expected, they were described in the 1912 annual report as "powerful." The *Dreadful's* boilers gave the ship a seventy-four nominal horsepower which is little more than a good-sized pleasure boat of today. In 1914 a fifth boat, the *Gleeful* was added to the fleet. The five tugs operated until 1916 when the British Admiralty commandeered the *Dreadful* for the war effort and the *Active* was purchased to replace her. The *Fearful* was disposed of in 1920 and *Active* remained in service until 1956 when under the flag of another firm she sank near Cortez Island. She was salvaged and the engine sold to a Victoria towing firm.

The company's first diesel-powered tugs, *Florence Filberg* and the *Mary Mackin* were purchased in 1946. *Isabella Stewart* was purchased a year later and renamed *Fraser Crown* in 1959. *Nootka Prince* was purchased that same year and renamed *Ocean Crown*. CZ now has three tugs and four barges in service.

Rayonier's boomman takes on a herding operation of cedar logs.

As with all improvements and progress, some of the fun and adventure also goes into history. But the oldtimers' stories live on to be retold many a time: one involves the day logging camp boss Max Elder, logger George Haywood and contractor Len Adcock nearly rode out to sea on a log raft. Elder, Haywood and Adcock were standing at the mouth of Muir Creek near Sooke trying to figure how to get an eight-section boom out of the creek mouth to a waiting tug through ground swells high as a house. Adcock said to Haywood: "Say, look George. Every seventh roller breaks flat, so why don't you get into that little old eighteen-foot, clinker built with the five-and-a-half horsepower motor and take out that towline, like a good chap?" Max Elder said he wouldn't blame anyone if they didn't want to go out in that weather and water. But he agreed they needed boom space and there were all those guys sitting around idle. Adcock had a contract and time was money and that tug had been sitting out there fuming and puffing for a long time. So he went out himself and, sure enough, he floated right over that seventh wave, hooked the tow cable to the bridle on the head stick and floated right back to the tug.

He was on his way home when the deckhand on the tug started to wave frantically. Seemed there was a short hauser in the clinkerbuilt that belonged on the tug. Adcock couldn't hear him above the surf and the motor. He couldn't quiet the surf but he could cut the motor, which he

Pretty as a picture but far more efficient is Haida Chieftain, *a Kingcome Navigation tug.*

did, then stood up, cupping his ears to hear better. A huge wave hit the boat and over the boat went like half an egg shell in a typhoon. He came up holding the keel in one hand and his bone-dry hat in the other. After a few minutes of helpless consternation, the deckhand lowered the tug's dinghy and oared his way towards Adcock in the pounding surf. A big wave hit the dinghy too and—in his efforts to hold on—the deckhand let go the oars, which went the way of all wood. Now there were two men out there in the chuck and no boats to rescue anyone. Max Elder had a bright idea: Since the boom had to be moved anyway, why not use it to pick up the drowning men? He told Haywood to cut all the tie-up lines with an axe, which he did, hacking through them like so many jungle vines. And the boom began to move, especially when it hit a freshet at the mouth of the creek. They hauled Adcock aboard and then the deckhand and his dinghy. And it was hunky dorey time.

Then somebody remembered that Adcock, Haywood and Elder were not scheduled to go to Vancouver on a log boom. By then that eight sections was really moving. Running over slippery logs that are ocean bound on a heavy surf is no easy task at any time and when Elder and Adcock reached the tail stick it was leaving the creek. But the water was only waist deep as they clambered onto dry ground. Haywood was farther back and when he jumped the water was swimming hole deep. "I never knew I could swim so well in caulk boots," he said later. He was congratulating himself on his aquatic abilities when Max Elder noticed that the swifter winch, on its own little platform, was still attached to the boom. (A swifter winch is used to haul "swifter sticks" across from the far side of the raft, over the mass of logs, where they are chained to brace the raft for towing.) "Since you're already wet, George, go out and cut that winch loose, please," Elder said in his kindest tone.

Haida Monarch makes inaugural log dump at Powell River harbor on her maiden voyage from the Queen Charlotte Islands in January, 1975. This was the world's first self-propelled, self-loading and self-dumping log carrier. A system of pumps and ballast tanks settles the vessel deep in the water then tilts it to port to slide the logs off the deck.

In August of 1960, Swiftsure Towing Company launched Forest Prince. *This was an innovation on the West Coast as the barge was both self-loading as well as self-dumping. With the continued expansion of the company, a second barge, the Swiftsure Prince was built and launched in 1970. Swiftsure is a wholly-owned subsidiary of British Columbia Forest Products with a fleet of four tugs and two log barges.*

194

Seaspan Forester *with a 20,000 ton load begins to tip.*

Seaspan Forester's *load begins to hit the water.*

Barge loader Howard Wilson operates loader that can pick up 35 tons of logs and swing them into position aboard the Alberni Carrier at Queen Charlotte Islands Division of MacMillan Bloedel.

Seaspan Forester *has swept the deck clean and is already starting to right herself.*

Island Sovereign, a Seaspan tug with 2,400 horsepower, tows the loaded Island Yarder at eight knots.

Luckily, there was a line aboard the floating platform and it was just long enough for the shorebound duo to loop it around a stump and pull Haywood and equipment back to shore. When Elder suggested a hot rum toddy might be in order, Haywood did not refuse. "I've been up and down this creek without a paddle all day," he said. "And enough is enough."

195

M.A. Grainger, Chief Forester, and J. Lathaue on inspection trip in May, 1914.

15.
The Protectors

B.C. Forest Service.

There's a very important segment of the forest industry story that must not be overlooked: the contribution of the British Columbia Forest Service. The protectors.

And there's a lot to protect. The ideal climatic and soil conditions essential for the rapid and abundant growth of big trees found in only a few regions of the entire world are available in British Columbia. Not only do our forests thrive in the moist and rugged coastal zone but also throughout most of the Interior. They grow in the lush valleys and they find adequate sustenance several thousand feet up the steep mountain slopes.

Of fifteen major commercial species found in the province's forests, most are coniferous, or needle-bearing. They grow tall, straight and thick. Although each type differs from the others in precise characteristics, all have some particularly good qualities which render them attractive for a wide variety of wood products—and these products are in great demand in many parts of the world. In short, the forest products industry is the backbone of British Columbia's economy, contributing approximately $2 billion in value annually and providing a livelihood for about 100,000 people, close to ten per cent of the Province's labor force. About seventy-five per cent of the British Columbia timber harvest is converted into lumber within the Province. This share has remained fairly constant over the last decade. During the same period pulp production has doubled.

The British Columbia Forest Service was formed after a Royal Commission Inquiry into the province's timber resources utilization, management, preservation, fire prevention and reforestation practices resulted in the Forest Act of 1912. The Service was set up as a branch of the provincial Department of Lands with responsibility for taking forest inventory, setting up fire fighting forces, developing

Roy Eden, 1920, just one of the dedicated rangers and wardens of the B.C. Forest Service who surveyed and patrolled the B.C. forests and helped end the "cut and get out" era.

lookout systems and—eventually—creating forest reserves, an ambitious project requiring ambitious men. The Inquiry of 1909 stated that Forest Rangers should be "thorough woodsmen and expert cruisers; they should be men with extensive practical experience of all local methods of logging and milling; they should be proficient in scaling." If that weren't enough, the Rangers also had to be "sound, sober and able-bodied, capable of enduring hardships and working under trying conditions in the open." Rangers were also supposed to be constables with the power to arrest offenders against the forest laws; they were also empowered to press men into service when necessary to fight forest fires.

Today there are about 100 dedicated Forest Rangers wearing numerous hats: managers of forest lands; firefighters; public relations men; policemen; engineers; office managers; resource planners and recreation officers. As manager of publicly owned (or Crown) land, a Forest Ranger's responsibilities include constant checks of volumes of wood being harvested, protection of the forest against fire and disease and reforestation matters. As a policeman he must know and enforce the Forest Act, the Anti-Litter Act and the Grazing Act. Ranger staff also carefully record the amount of acreage disturbed by mining exploration work and bill the companies for timber and other losses.

Gerry Wellburn, pioneer lumberman and collector of vintage logging equipment, stands at the base of a fir tree that measures nine feet in diameter and rises 150 feet to the first limb.

Mount Glory lookout shelter with Assistant Ranger Noakes and lookout man Hewitt in August, 1928. Mt. Glory is south of the Blueberry-Paulson Highway in the Nancy Green, Christina Lake areas.

An old Barton portable pump run off a vintage automobile was the way some firefighting was done in the Twenties.

Blue River Ranger Station in the Kamloops District. Is that a wash basin or dog dish outside the cabin door?

Forest Service cabin at Summit Lake, north of Prince George, built in 1923. Six District Foresters today administer a like number of Forest Districts: Vancouver, Prince Rupert, Prince George, Kamloops, Nelson and Cariboo.

Mouse Mountain lookout built by Rangers Eden, Madeau and Susage using timbers cut on the site and hauled by horses. Mouse Mountain is southeast of 10 Mile Lake in Cariboo District.

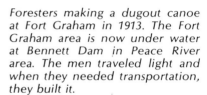

Foresters making a dugout canoe at Fort Graham in 1913. The Fort Graham area is now under water at Bennett Dam in Peace River area. The men traveled light and when they needed transportation, they built it.

By the time the Forest Act of 1912 had been passed, timber harvesting on a haphazard, wasteful basis had been going on for fifty years. The abundant forests were considered a nuisance by many pioneers and early loggers, who cleared away trees to get the land for farming; large tracts of timbered land were sold to private interests. In 1896 initial regulations were expanded and the sale of forested land along with harvesting rights was prohibited.

The Forest Service is responsible to the British Columbia Minister of Lands, Forests and Water Resources and consists of thirteen separate divisions, each with a different jurisdiction. Administration of the Service is headed by a Deputy Minister, Chief Forester, two Assistant Chief Foresters (one responsible for operations and one for resource management) and a Director of Services. Six District Foresters administer that number of Forest Districts: Vancouver, Prince Rupert, Prince George, Kamloops, Nelson and Cariboo. They contain over 100 Ranger Districts.

Productive forest land in British Columbia is harvested under various licences, leases and contracts from the "Crown"—a term meaning the public or state. One of these is the Tree Farm Licence, a twenty-one year contract permitting the holder to harvest timber on a specified unit of land with the responsibility of managing the land on a Sustained Yield Basis. Logging must be carried out according to a systematic plan subject to approval by the Service; close utilization standards must be met; logged over lands must be reforested and the holder of a Tree Farm Licence is responsible for fire prevention and suppression. Public Sustained Yield Units (PSYU) are areas of timbered land, usually defined by natural topographic features such as rivers or mountain ranges, managed by government and logged under short term licences by a number of operators whose collective cut cannot exceed the annual allowable cut for the unit. An important section of the Forest Service is the Inventory Division which is responsible for regularly taking stock of the Province's wood volume. Such inventory is carried out on a continuing basis with reports handed down every ten years. The first such catalogue was completed in 1957; the amount of annual allowable cuts of the PSYU are determined from these inventory reports.

199

Forest companies also take part in seeding and reforestation of logged over land. A MacMillan Bloedel employee has just planted a Douglas fir for next century's crop.

D.F. Marvin and rangers Sharkey and Bonney and forest guard Little at Quesnel in 1914. Rangers enforce Grazing Act, Anti-Litter Act and the Forest Act, which was legislated in 1912.

B.C. Forest Service employee inspects seedlings grown in plastic containers for "bullet" planting. Scene is Duncan nursery on Vancouver Island.

Reforestation is another of the Service's divisions and one of the most vital. Beginning with the start of the first nursery in 1927, through a period of sporadic attempts at artificial reseeding and a long period of relying on natural regeneration, this division has evolved into a major and integral part of forest management. With the advent of Tree Farm Licences in the Forties, industry was required to plant their logged over areas. All the seed collected from their own areas and that from Provincial forests is processed and tested by the Forest Service and grown in the Service's eight nurseries. The target to produce 75 million trees in 1975 was already surpassed in 1974 and in future the Service and the logging firms expect there will be sufficient trees grown to keep up with the demands for reforesting logged or burned areas and catching up on areas that have been left unplanted in the past. Of all the trees grown in the nurseries, the Forest Service is planting about fifty per cent on Crown forest areas while industry is planting the remainder on areas for which they are responsible. Seed collection is an important aspect of this program. As with any elementary breeding plan, only seeds from carefully selected stock are collected to ensure improved crops. After picking, seed cones are sent to the seed extraction plant at Duncan on Vancouver Island where seeds are extracted and stored in special freezer units for up to several years.

Infant seedlings are carefully nurtured for two years when they are considered ready for planting. Planting can be done by several methods including the bare root system which means digging a small hole in the ground, inserting the seedling and packing the earth firmly around it. The mud pack method involves encasing a root of field grown tree in a clay-peat mixture allowing package insertion in "dibble holes"; the plug method uses a planting "gun" to insert one-year-old seedlings grown in plastic containers into the ground. The gun is designed to split the casing at the time of insertion to free the roots; the plug method is similar to the mud pack method except that the one year old seedling is grown in a styrofoam casing in well fertilized soil. Before planting, the seedlings are removed from their casing and inserted in dibble holes.

MacMillan Bloedel worker fills up sacks with newly picked pine cones and attaches a label signifying the species.

B.C. Forest Service field at Duncan, on Vancouver Island.

Norm Crist shoots down seedlings for transplanting purposes. The action took place at Rayonier's Port McNeill division.

Norm Crist examines his quarry, a seedling, that he has just shot down with a .22 rifle for transplanting at Rayonier's Port McNeill location.

Kathy Hanson, Norm Crist, Miriam Doroghty doing reforestation chores for Rayonier.

About 110,000 acres are now being replanted each year by the Forest Service and by industry. Trees mature at different rates depending on tree variety, soil and climatic conditions; in some areas a stand of trees is considered mature at about eighty years while in others 350 years may be required to produce a mature tree. During the growing period, pruning of underbranches and thinning of trees may be carried out to improve the quality and quantity of timber. Care is also taken to avoid conditions that breed insects or create fire hazards. The Protection Division of the Forest Service is devoted to coordination of forest fire fighting and fighting and prevention of disease and insect infestation. Forest fires annually raze an average of 325,000 acres of timber, killing not only trees but resident wildlife. These figures are based on the years 1968 to 1972. Cost to the taxpayer of fighting forest fires in 1973 alone was about $8.7 million.

MacMillan Bloedel forestry worker gathering cones for next century's harvest.

Janet Massey of Rayonier takes part in many reforestation duties as well as scaling for Rayonier.

Approximately forty per cent of the fires in British Columbia are caused by lightning. The remainder are the result of man's influence on the environment—whether the result of industrial operations or the recreationist. The Forest Service seeks to eliminate the man-made fires through educational programs in industry and the community. It has an extensive public relations department geared to inform public, press and industry through the use of films, slides, publications, news releases and other materials. The Service has a very effective fire control program consisting of a network of over one hundred and twenty lookout towers complemented by an efficient communications system and air patrols. Also, a number of protective measures are taken, including the restriction of forest access land during periods of high fire hazard.

Vernon fire area caused by lightning in 1952. Over the past ten years there was an average of 2,410 forest fires per year, of which 36.6 per cent were caused by lightning.

Not a pretty sight is a burned out logging area. Such locations are now being gradually planted with new stock which will be the forest crop for citizens of 2000 A.D.

Faculty of Forestry students from UBC measuring slash for Rayonier.

Lynda Pendergast of MacMillan Bloedel's Northwest Bay Division with a Douglas fir seedling about to be entered in a race for survival. Until about 30 or 40 years ago both the Forest Service and industry relied entirely on natural regeneration for the development of new growth on logged or burned-over forest land. This is no longer so.

Fireweed takes over from the fire after a slash burn in Nimpkish area. In years gone by, fires have often proved to be nature's way of clearing up old, decadent, diseased and infested forests so that vigorous new growth could start again.

Elk Lake fire on the edge of Reginald Lake, south of Campbell Lake on Vancouver Island. The average area annually burned is 229,487 acres with cost of fighting fires more than three million dollars a year.

Snag fallers will come in after a forest fire and cut dangerous snags like these down. In Vancouver Forest District a total of 1,877 acres was felled in 1973. Of that, 650 acres was by contract and 1,227 acres by the District snag-falling crew. In Cariboo District, 400 acres of snags were felled by the Forest Service.

The 1959 Mt. Brenton burn, southwest of Chemainus. Fire detection and reporting have been improving as time goes on. To augment the lookout towers and normal public reporting systems, air patrols over areas of high fire-probability are carried out.

Port Neville fire on June 25, 1925. Loggers can be seen fleeing at height of blaze.

Slash burning is a controversial subject but a study conducted after the infamous Eden forest fire of Sept. 11, 1973, by Dr. D.B. Turner, former B.C. Deputy Minister of Recreation and Conservation, agreed that it would be against the best interests of the province to ban slash burning and that a major initiative was required to develop the understanding of how, when and where slash burning should be conducted.

Canso airtanker drops its water load on a Maple Bay fire in 1969. Aircraft and helicopters play increasingly important roles by bombing fires with water and special fire retardants as well as transporting men and equipment to fire areas.

Once a fire has started the fighting forces go into action against it. All techniques, from sophisticated machinery right down to hand-wielded tools are thrown into the battle. The Service uses air tankers to drop a mixture of fire retardant and chemical and water (or plain water) on the fire. Other types of aircraft are used to deliver men and equipment to the scene. These men may be a regular Forest Service fire suppression crew, an industry crew or a crew of volunteers who have registered with the Ranger in that area. Bulldozers are also recruited to help clear areas to create fire "breaks". Men using shovels, axes, power-saws, and even brooms, further clear the ground to bare earth to provide an effective break. Portable pumps and thousands of feet of hose transport water to the site for use in the fight. But even with all the new equipment, firefighting is a hot, dirty, eye-stinging task for the ground crew—and a dangerous one.

Forests provide more than wood products and jobs to the citizens of British Columbia. For recreationists there are nearly 9 million acres of Provincial and Federal parks in British Columbia and, of this, nearly 4 million acres are productive forest land. It is one of the reasons why tourists visit British Columbia; tourism is the Province's second largest industry.

Fire line looking north from Mesachie Mountain in Lake Cowichan area.

The Forest Service and the forest industries have taken several significant steps towards opening the forest to the public. Without the logging industry, most of the Province's public roads, particularly on Vancouver Island, would not be there at all. Recently the British Columbia Government set aside 2,200 small, carefully selected receational reserves. Many are quite remote, but they have been "put in the bank" for the future and will be developed as they become more accessible and as the demand requires. The Government has also established 100 ecological reserves throughout the Province. In them the natural ecological processes will be free to continue without the consequence of man's intrusion.

Thanks to the foresight of our forefathers over fifty years ago in establishing the British Columbia Forest Service, we have an organization charged with the task of checking man's natural greed to ensure that the forests' rewards will be preserved in perpetuity.

Getting there and getting back was part of the day's event for men riding the "speeder". This early variety was run by Merrill & Ring at Squamish in 1926.

Big man, big trees. Gordon Flowerdew of Beaver Cove and Englewood helped fall some of these forest giants. Gordon didn't like the loggers being separated from the rest of the passengers on the trips "to town."

16.
Going To Town

When the loggers "went to town", they really did.

In the old days, even today, when a logger spoke of "going to town", he meant Vancouver. Although almost every weekend the thunder of caulk boots used to echo through the streets of Nanaimo (which had an infamous Red Light district), Port Alberni and other communities on the fringes of the big camps, Vancouver was the preferred destination of the logger who was either "stakey" or "bushed." He would get on one of the Union, CPR or Northland Navigation ships and steam towards the big city with a head of steam of his own—one that he'd built up on the boat.

Where did the liquor come from? Jack Bell, recently retired manager of Northwest Bay Division of MacMillan Bloedel said there was little hard drinking in the camps in the 1930s because the bullbucker was there to take liquor off the loggers when they got to camp. "I always gave it back to them when they left for town," Bell said. "I can remember having seven or eight cases of booze stacked up in my office at Franklin River." This cached booty was put to good use on the way to town so the loggers were well into their cups by the time they hit the quayside.

Some camps had very rudimentary wharves; some had none so the logger escaping for his trip to town had to literally jump aboard on the run. Alighting was the same: leaping off, sometimes into a waiting skiff, other times onto a log boom, often after dark. He might fall into the chuck. "It wasn't so bad in coming back," one former logger said. "You were usually broke anyway. But you didn't want to fall in going because you had your good clothes on and money in your pocket."

"We've got 150 loggers and fifty passengers," the radio operator on the *Maquinna* used to tell his Vancouver office, depending on the quantity stated on the manifest. "That really used to bug me, separating us like we were a bunch of animals," said CANFOR's Gordon Flowerdew.

What the well-dressed logger wore in 1911. This chap had just knocked over a big one in the Ocean Falls area.

207

Now employed as recreation and fire safety director at Woss Camp, Flowerdew said it was unfair to label all loggers as heavy drinkers and womanizers. Nevertheless, they were a breed apart, whether they wanted to be or not. And every known kind of freeloader and vice merchant was waiting at dockside to help separate a logger from his hard earned money. Not that some needed much help. They threw it away on whiskey in hotel rooms, beer in the beer parlors and on cheap women or prostitutes. If they didn't get "rolled" in a cheap hotel by some tramp, they would lend large portions to other loggers looking for a "drag," or loan against the day when they would have to give up their holiday away from the woods.

The trips down on the boats were boisterous affairs as loggers met old friends from other camps and generally let go months of pent-up frustrations. Those they did not meet going down they found in the "loggers' hotels": the Belmont, Abbotsford, Europe, West, Lotus, York, Castle, Martin (now the Blackstone), Patricia and others in downtown Vancouver. A logger always stayed at the same hotel. It was logical, "you could always find a friend at the place he used when he was in town," says Sam Hardy, railroad foreman at Woss Camp. Also, the hotel manager or desk clerk would forward or hold a logger's mail and look after his messages until he got settled. Some even left their "good clothes" at the hotel for the clerk to send out for cleaning. When they came to town for the next fray, they'd be there waiting, pressed, stains removed. The loggers got to know their hotelmen so well they could hit them for a drag. That was always the first debt to be paid once the logger was back at work.

A lot of city logging got done in the beer parlors. At noon on almost any day there would be a dozen men at a table and by two or three o'clock there would be as many as thirty or more serious drinkers at a cluster of tables. When he wasn't gulping the beer as fast as the pot-bellied, sweating waiter in the stained white, open-necked shirt could bring them, the logger on holiday was eating steak at the Fish & Oyster Bar, Scott's, Clancy's Sky Diner or The Skillet on Granville Street. Some might find their way to the restaurant at the Stanley, the Lotus or the old Vancouver Hotel, but if a logger's budget was slim, he might be found at the Shasta Cafe on Hastings Street, a number of other places in Chinatown, or on the skidroad.

Some fights took place. Some were continuations of those started earlier at Nanaimo, Port Alberni, Duncan or elsewhere on the Island. "There used to be some great brawls in the old days between loggers from different camps," said Jack Bell. "And then there were coal miners. That made for some real good donnybrooks. Sunday morning we'd get a call from the police saying that part or all of our crew was in jail. The police would give us a sum total of bail, fines and damages; we'd put a cheque in the mail and the crew would be back in time for work on Monday morning."

Canadian Forest Products at one time hired a Union steamship to transport between four and five hundred loggers back to camp. "You can imagine the kind of shape some of them were in by the time they got back after thirty-six hours of boozing on that boat," says Jack Vetleson. "We had to pack some of 'em off on stretchers to get 'em on the speeder and back to camp."

Scarred veteran of many a tug-o-war with the donkey and the logs being yarded in is this tree at Brooks, Scanlon & O'Brian at Stillwater, 1926. Man is unidentified. B., S. & O. were taken over by Matt Hemmingsen who sold to British Columbia Forest Products.

The going back was a difficult decision. And after it had been delayed as long as possible, there were logging agencies on Abbott Street and Carrall Street that helped you make the choice. One such agency in 1911 had this warning posted on the wall:

"All fees must be paid in advance. Do not ask for credit. Every man hired here must report within time stated on the contract. No fees refunded to drunks or those who miss train or boat. Any man refusing to go where hired must forfeit all fees paid. No fee refunded in any case unless you bring a statement signed by your employer. Do not represent to be what you are not as your employer will soon find out and you will not get any more work from this office."

Fraser's logging camp in the 1880s or earlier. After a day of working in these conditions, a romp into town would have been nice. It wasn't likely, however. Notice the height of the stumps.

Building a bridge on the skidroad at the Hastings Sawmill Company camp on Thurlow Island. Anyone for a cool beer?

George Smythe, IWA Local 1-80 President from 1956 to 1960 recalls there was a Vancouver hiring agency called Joy's, and another called Hick's "where you could buy a job if you bought a bottle for them." Those loggers who were welcomed back to their old jobs didn't have to bother with agencies. But they found it hard to resist the "man-catcher". This individual was the forerunner of today's personnel manager, although he had more of the characteristics of a one-man press gang of the sort that used to Shanghai ship's crews. Most big camps had them. The man-catcher would operate in the beer parlors, hiding place for most of his victims. He would walk into the beer parlor and head straight for the table with the largest, thirstiest occupants, confident that it would be surrounded by loggers, and then ask for a man by name. "Oh, he's over at the Dufferin," somebody would tattletale. Or, "I seen him at noon with Joe Skouse down at the Austin." The man-catcher would be off to round up his man with a combination of persuasion, threats, a bribe of $50 advance money and a bottle of rye to see him through the dry spell on the way home.

Chaser pulls on the strawline at a Rayonier camp. Loggers today can have a noggin of grog in the camp or get to town in a few hours, if they really want to go.

Going back was as boisterous as going down because the loggers knew it would be a long time until they got out again. The difference was, he may have gone out stakey but he often came back shakey. For many, the woods was a place to dry out. "I remember one time, coming

209

back, this old hooktender—an awful man to drink—came up to me on the boat," Jack Vetleson said. "He'd set chokers for me at Rock Bay years ago and he says: 'you must have a bottle somewhere, Jack'. Well, I had a bottle in the suitcase but I didn't want to give it to him because I wasn't going to do him a favor by giving him a drink. Anyway, I got tired of him bugging me so I finally got an empty bottle and filled it with tap water and said, 'Here, Bill, have a drink.' He grabbed that bottle and tipped it up and then he put it down and said 'water' in the dirtiest way I ever heard anybody say anything. I never knew you could say 'water' and make it sound like a swear word!"

But some loggers managed to get their liquor supply back to camp regardless of eagle-eyed supervisors. Most times a logger had to bring bottles for friends in camp, friends who'd say to him the moment he arrived: "You want me to carry your suitcase for you?" Or: "Did you wanna see me before supper?", a password for, "where's the liquor?" Loggers could spot a fellow woodsman a block away just by the way he walked, particularly if he was carrying his suitcase in his arms, like a baby. His armful was just as precious to him, but it wasn't only because of its valuable cargo that he carried it that way. The handles had long ago broken off because it was so frequently overloaded.

On the way home the noisy revelers were given a wide berth by the "passengers", although it was an unwritten law that loggers never bothered women or children. One such trip stays in the mind of Chuck Horel, now a successful Salt Spring Island realtor. He was travelling on the *Maquinna* in the spring of 1934 when a group of American tourists, "good and proper souls all of them" teased him into reciting a "logger-Chinook" jingle. "A Seattle school teacher was to interpret for them," Horel said. "I was just a logging camp urchin at the time but I had quite a repertoire of jingles and ballads of mixed English-Chinook crudity that would make even our present day college seniors blush. Anyway . . . The school teacher, a decent chap, interpreted. And when I finished he hustled me out of the lounge and gave me four bits and advised me strongly to forget the ballad. That was a lot of money in those days and it must have worked because all I can recollect of that offending recitation is the refrain:

"There's hiyu clams and mowitch and klootchmen by the way.
Delate tennass moosem while the twilight fades away."

Mr Horel said his memory might be faulty but he was told later that the couplet he sang at that time translated roughly as: "Then we'll have a little sex after the girls have served the chowder."

Before leaving the loggers' social life for other topics, it should not be forgotten that there were many communities where nightlife on Saturday was more readily available, places where a community hall or recreation centre was the scene of a well-attended Saturday night dance.

The logger came in wearing his uniform: dark grey or blue suit, pointed city shoes, white socks with lots of hairy leg showing when he sat down, white shirt, and a tie with red in it. The women were feminine in flowered catalogue dresses. There was no drinking in the hall so the men took generous swigs from bottles in brown paperbags in parked cars. The women headed for the kitchen, a cold, vee-jointed,

A little change of pace at International Timber Company, Campbell River camp in 1926. The bottle feeding seems to fascinate two youngsters who can still remember when they got their sustenance the same way.

damp-smelling portion of the building where CPR style crockery, blue-rimmed and chipped, stood on badly painted shelves and oilcloth covered tables. A huge wood stove commanded one corner, its ornate wrought iron legs splayed. Flycatchers, black with last summer's rewards held in a sticky embrace, hung from the ceiling. Children ran around the hall and into the kitchen, playing tag and screaming and being screamed back at by mothers and others. The women were distracted; they had one eye on the kids and the other on the man they were with. "I hope Jerry doesn't drink too much," a young one would confide. The youngest children soon grew tired and cranky and had to be taken out to the car and put to sleep. The older children, finally exhausted, bedded themselves down on long benches around the walls. Some fell asleep across a mass of boots and overshoes and fallen coats in the cloakroom.

Chokerman kicking hole under the log. Maybe he was going to get a whole sackful of chokerholes for the hooktender?

The music by the local "band"—a piano, fiddle, harmonica or accordion, forced out a schottische, heel and toe polka or Paul Jones. The men, surprisingly agile (surprising only to those who don't know how agile you have to be to work in the woods), worked just as hard at dancing as anything else they did and the hall soon resounded with music and thumping feet.

Completely unheeded, the smell of fresh sandwiches and coffee wafted in from the kitchen. The gaiety of the scene was only occasionally marred by fights at the doorway and on the steps. Sometimes it was over a woman, but if it was a lifetime grudge, the combatants went behind the hall to straighten things out once and for all. Very often the two returned with their arms around each other, swearing lifelong friendship. The RCMP, and the Provincial Police before them, were discreetly aware of the goings-on at the hall, including the drinking in cars, but unless there were under-agers involved, they usually stayed clear of anything short of a full-scale riot.

The logger, formerly resplendent in his best clothes, already described, had undergone a transformation: straight rum or rye out of the bagged container had reddened his complexion and the color had been heightened by dancing. His tie had long since been removed—it was only a badge to get him in the door and to please the wife or girlfriend any way—and the white shirt was opened at the neck displaying a vast muscular chest.

The music quickened. Somebody fell down, made unsteady by over-indulgence. Others stayed remarkably sober and danced every dance with every woman in the place including grandmothers and blushing twelve year olds. At dawn the dance was over and even the hardiest survivors found it difficult to foxtrot without music, the band having left two hours earlier.

The weekly newspaper gave the event a glowing report in its social column. "A good time was had by all," it read. And it was.

It was great fun "going to town" but it was a drag getting back. There is some feeling of isolation still in logging camps. This young logger is seeing the Rayonier "crummy", sea division, head off from Sewell Inlet, Queen Charlotte Islands.

211

The way it was . . . Cowichan Bay Regatta 1910.

Obstacle power bucking is demonstrated here by Al Boyko of MB's Sproat Lake Logging Division at Alberni Loggers' sports.

Ed Marcellus doing the standing block chop at PNE.

Jim Shillito of MB's Franklin River Division leans into saw at Alberni loggers' sports.

17.
The Sporting Life
Loggers prove they can have fun too.

When loggers work, they work hard. And when they play, they play hard too. Anyone who has witnessed a loggers' sports day can tell you that. At a dozen far-flung logging camps, loggers can be found every year putting on climbing spurs and sharpening saws and axes for games of skill that include everything from racing up spar trees to setting chokers and throwing axes. They're also sharpening up skills that—in some cases—are no longer required in the modern logging camp. The loggers' sports shows are preserving, in one sense, the disappearing talents of the pioneer woodsman.

Modern logging skills are included too, with several events included at every sports day. Some of these sports days are held at the big camps—like those at CANFOR's Woss Camp and Rayonier's Mahatta River where the whole logging community turns out for a full day of activities. Others are held in urban centres and are part of a larger scene: Vancouver's Pacific National Exhibition, Victoria's Victorian Days, Sooke's All Sooke Day and the Sports Day at Port Alberni. Some, but not all, sports days are sanctioned by The Canadian Loggers' Sports Association (CANLOG) which was formed in 1969 as part of the Festival of Forestry, a promotional umbrella for the British Columbia forest industry. As the Festival grew, so did the interest in loggers' sports since one of its features is the big show at the PNE. Two other shows were also held at Sooke and at Squamish.

Sooke is the grandfather of all loggers' shows (started in 1934) and is the home of Jube and Ardy Wickheim, world champion log birlers for ten years. Interest in loggers' sports has increased to the degree that Jube Wickheim now employs about twenty men on an annual basis staging logging demonstrations throughout North America, Japan,

Logging was never like this!

213

Australia and New Zealand. Areas wishing CANLOG sanctions have to meet a strict set of safety standards and rules before insurance will be issued to competitors. In 1974 CANLOG sanctioned fourteen events in British Columbia and the national championships in Toronto. More than $80,000 was offered in prize money. In 1973, Jube Wickham led a twelve-man delegation to Tasmania where a World Loggers' Sport organization was formed. At that meeting, thirteen world championship events were won by Canada. In 1971, the Provincial Government, recognizing the contribution loggers' sports was making towards creating an awareness of loggers as athletes, proclaimed loggers' sports as the official industry sport of British Columbia.

The Festival of Forestry, which is supported by the three levels of government, the International Woodworkers of America, suppliers to the logging industry and the Council of Forest Industries, then embarked on a program to take a group of educators and loggers on a tour of Quebec's forests to acquaint British Columbians with the Quebec industry and to introduce loggers' sports there. A similar tour was organized for Ontario which met with equal success and led to the establishment of the Ontario Loggers' Sports Association.

"We have come a long way," said Bill Moore, chairman of the Festival of Forestry and CANLOG. "The men of our forests are part of a great community of people, living in camps with their families, dedicated to an industry with which they are prospering. Loggers' sports are a vehicle to tell this story."

Setting chokers is all in a day's fun at Mahatta River Loggers' Day.

Nice day for a swim. Log birling action at the PNE loggers' sports.

Throwing the axe at Mahatta River Sports Day.

At Mahatta River, even the ladies get into the action.

This logger at PNE gets a little help from the man with the oil can as he leans into the crosscut.

No matter how you look at it, it's a long way to the top.

Greased pole climbers at Mahatta River Sports Day, a Rayonier event.

Now that's stagged off pants! Chopping action at PNE loggers' sports events.

Barrelling right along are these barefoot boys with cheek. Rayonier camp at Mahatta River.

215

Anchor Stump: Stumps to which guy, or high lead lines are attached.

Arch: Heavy steel frame shaped like an inverted "U", each leg of which rides upon a set of tractor treads or wheels. Coupled to a tractor, it supports one end of the logs being hauled to a landing.

Asparagus: A bundle of small logs strapped together for easier handling between woods and pulp mill; especially useful when the logs are towed as the method prevents them from spreading all over the river.

Bag Boom: Logs in water surrounded by boomsticks in circle.

Bean Burner: A camp cook, usually not a good one. A Can Opener Artist is another of the same ilk.

Bedroll: Oldtime loggers used to pack their own bedroll or bedding from camp to camp. It usually consisted of a couple of bug-infested blankets.

Bight: Being in one can be dangerous. It is the area within the curve of any diverted line and since lines under tension have a way of striahgtening themselves up unexpectedly, loggers are warned to "stay out of the bight".

Bird Dog: A small plane used in firefighting to guide waterbombers over target area.

Block: A pulley sheave and its housing used to guide wire ropes.

Boom Chain: Chain used in securing logs in a boom.

Boom: Logs in water ready to tow to mill; river operation where logs are sorted and made into rafts to be towed to destination.

Boomman: The worker who performs the function of sorting the logs in a boom. He uses a pike pole, a long aluminum pole with a tipped end that can be used to push or pull logs into place.

Boomstick: A long, thin log used crossways in booming logs. Has an auger hole at either end; chained in series they enclose the booming grounds and provide framework for booms.

Brow Log: A log to protect log cars at spar tree.

Bucker: Member of cutting crew who saws felled trees into logs of designated lengths.

Bull Car: A big flat car used to move donkey engine.

Bullcook: A man who cuts wood, cleans up bunkhouses and does assorted duties around logging camp.

Bullchoker: Heavy chain choker used when extra strength is needed to move heavy log or to overcome bad hangup.

Bulldozer: Attachment to tractor for moving earth or other material; term is now used to described the vehicle as well.

Bull of the Woods: Logging superintendent.

Bull Pen: An area where unsorted logs are dumped.

Bull Team: Team of oxen used in early logging in British Columbia and coastal United States.

Bunk: Log rest on railway car or truck.

Butt Rigging: Connecting device between choker and main line; short length of cable equipped with swivel, clevises and butt hooks.

Cat: Caterpillar tractor.

Cat Doctor: Tractor mechanic.

Cat Side: A logging operation where a cat is used to bring logs to the landing.

216

Catskinner: Tractor driver.

Caulk: Pronounced "cork". Steel pegs in soles of logger's boots to ensure a safer footing in the woods.

Chaser: Worker who unhooks chokers at landing.

Cherry Picker: Machine for picking up lost logs on a railway.

Choker: Short length of wire rope, one end of which is noosed around log and other end attached to main line or butt rigging.

Chokerhole: Sometimes it is necessary to dig a hole under log in order to get choker around it. This is the chokerhole.

Chokerman or Choker Setter: Worker who places chokers around logs preparatory to yarding them to landing.

Glossary

Chuck: The sea. Salt Chuck.

Claim: Timbered country surveyed for logging by a company.

Cold Deck: Pile of logs yarded together for loading or storage.

Cord: Cubic measure for wood equal to eight feet long, four feet high and four feet wide.

Crock: A bottle, usually containing spirits.

Cruiser: Worker who inventories volume and grade of standing timber.

Crummy: Car or bus to transport logging crews to work area. In railroad show, an enclosed conveyance used for the same purpose.

Cunit: A measure of wood volume: 100 cubic feet.

Donkey Engine: Evolved from crude steam rigs, portable gasoline or diesel engine equipped with drums and cables used to move logs from woods.

Donkey Puncher: Donkey engineer.

Fake: A gasoline donkey.

Faller: Member of the cutting crew who cuts down trees.

Falling: Process of falling or harvesting trees.

Fore & Aft: Road of logs laid end to end.

Flunkey: A table waiter, waitress, dishwasher, or both, in a logging camp.

Flume: A wooden trough on trestles used to carry logs to dump. Just a memory, although traces of them can still be found in logging areas.

Gin Pole: Short spar tree for loading.

Grub: Food.

Guthammer: Dinner gong. In old days it was usually a triangular piece of metal which the cook would hit with a chunk of iron to announce mealtimes.

Guy Line: Wire rope attached to and stretched between stump or ground anchor and a pole, tree or tower to hold them firmly in place.

Gyppo: A small logging operator or contractor. Term is also used to define such an operation.

Hangfire: A dynamite charge that fails to blow in the normal time required for the fuse to blow down. Dynamite was used in logging camps to clear rock for roads, to break up log jams and, occasionally, to top a spar tree.

Hangup: A turn of logs fouled up in a root, snag or stump.

217

Hand Feller: Early logger who cut trees down with an axe and crosscut saw. He was also a Hand Logger.

Haulback: Line attached to end of main line which returns main line and chokers to woods from landing.

Haywire Show: A logging operation without safety standards. Dangerous place to work.

Heel Boom: Loading rig used in days of spar tree. Logs were caught by the loading tongs and the one end was lifted against the "heel" of fore-section of the loading boom giving the engineer leverage control to swing them onto truck.

Highball: Go ahead fast. A hustle outfit.

High Lead: System of yarding logs from cutting area to landing using lifting power of high rigged cables to move logs up and over obstructions. Use spar tree.

High Lead Block: Large steel pulley strapped to top of spar tree for carrying main line.

Hogan's Alley: Wooden walkway between bunkhouses and wash house.

Hog: Locomotive.

Hogger: Engineer of locomotive.

Hooktender: Foreman over a high lead "side"; supervises all operations of yarding and loading.

Inkslinger: Timekeeper or office worker.

Jam: Log jam; pileup of logs in a river drive.

Jersey Cream: Extra good timber.

Jill Poke: A log unloading device.

Landing: A cleared area to which logs are yarded from the woods to be loaded onto trucks.

Locie: Locomotive.

Log Dump: End of road where logs are put in water.

Main Line: Large cable used to yard logs from cutting area to landing and to which chokers are attached.

Man-catcher: A company representative whose job it was to induce holidaying loggers to return to camp.

Mfbm: A measure of lumber recoverable from logs: thousand foot board measure.

Mulligan Mixer: Head cook.

Molly Hogan: No relation to Hogan of Hogan's Alley. A link made of wire strands.

Needle Fire: A very light burn which only singes the needles off the slash.

Nose Bag Show: A camp where a lunchbucket is carried.

Nut Splitter: Locomotive mechanic.

Peeler: Logs suitable for peeling into veneer for plywood.

Pile or Piling: Log driven vertically into ground, usually to secure a pier or dock.

Piledriver: Machine for driving piles.

Pot: Steam logging donkey.

Powder Monkey: Worker who uses dynamite in logging operation.

Purchase: A good steady pull, using blocks.

Raft: A boom of logs, such as in Davis Raft, Canadian invention for moving logs in heavy seas.

Rigger: If "high rigger", man who tops spar tree and rigs it. Can mean head man on a skidder show—also "skidder"

Rigging: Lines, hooks, etc. Fittings. Also means to get the spar tree ready for use in yarding.

Rigging Crew: Rigs tower or spar tree and brings in logs. Consists of hooktender, rigging slinger, choker setters, whistle punk and chaser.

Rigging Slinger: Supervises and works with chokerman and signalman (formerly work done by whistlepunk) in cutting area. Selects logs to be yarded, untangles rigging, directs signalman to transmit signals to yard operator or signals himself with radio whistle.

Roll: Rob of money. A fairly frequent occurrence in days when "stakey" loggers hit town and met the wrong kind of women.

Saw Log: Log suitable for manufacturing into lumber.

Scaler: Measures each bucked log for number of board feet and grade. Uses scale stick or calipers and steel tape.

Schoolmarm: Tree with a large fork.

Show: The area being logged.

Side: A yarding unit. Can mean complete yarding, loading, falling and bucking crew.

Skyline: Heavy cable hung between two spar trees with a traveling carriage to haul logs through the air in rough country.

Skidroad: Roadway along which logs were dragged by bulls, later, horses, then machine donkeys; also refers to area of city where some loggers congregate. *Not* skidrow—in logger terminology, there is no such place.

Slash: A logged off area. Also means to cut a line through bush for a survey crew.

Snag: A dead tree.

Snoose: Chewing tobacco, the constant companion of the oldtime logger. Also used in expression: "Give 'er snoose!", meaning, "Let 'er rip!" "Highball!".

Snooser: Derogatory term to describe Scandinavian logger.

Spar Tree: Tree topped and limbed for use in high lead logging.

Speeder: A railcar with a motor used on railway track; large varieties were railroad version of crummy and used to transport workers to job site.

Springboard: Board oldtime fallers stood on to fall trees.

Stakey: Term used to define a logger who had made a "stake". When he got stakey it was time to "go to town".

Strap: Short length of wire rope with an eye or splice or socket on each end by which blocks are attached to trees or logs.

Straw Line: A small line used to pull heavier lines.

Stumpage: Standing merchantable timber. Can also denote price paid for timber.

Suicide Show: A dangerous piece of ground to log.

Sustained Yield: Cutting no more timber than nature can replace by growth.

Tail Block: Pulley attached to anchor stump through which a cable passes and used to return mainline and chokers to cutting area.

Tin Pants: Water repellant trousers.

Turn: The group of logs being yarded to the landing at any one time.

Undercut: Notch cut in tree to regulate direction of tree fall.

Whistle Punk: Signalman. Transmits signals by electric buzzer or horn to yarding engine to indicate movements of rigging in yarding logs.

Windfall: Tree that has fallen from force of wind.

Widow-maker: A loose limb or tree that has fallen into another tree which, if it falls on a logger, can make a widow of his wife.

Woods: A term used in the West to mean timber country, logging area. "Bush" is also used to mean the same place.

Wolf Tree: A large tree that hogs the sunlight.

Yarding: Process of hauling logs by high lead or tractor from cutting area to landing.

Photo Credits

Photographs are described from left to right and top to bottom for each page. AR, Artray; BC, British Columbia Archives; BF, Bud Frost; BJ, B. C. Jennings; BK, Brian Kyle; CF, Council of Forest Industries; CI, Commercial Illustrators; CP, Catto and Pierson; CS, Croton Studios; CZ, Crown Zellerbach; DL, Dave Loog; DR, Dave Roels; DT, B.C. Department to Travel; DU, Dunning Hoff; EG, Ed Gould; FP, B.C. Forest Products; FS, B.C. Forest Service; FW, F. W. Lees; GB, Gennie Beardsley; GG, Grant Garnett; GI, Graphic Industries; GN, Geo. N. Y. Simpson; JC, Jack Cash; JG, J. G. Gibson; JL, Jack Lindsay; MB, MacMillan Bloedel; MK, Martin Keeley; MM, Mike McQuarrie; NF, National Film Board; NY, Nick Yunge-Bateman; OB, O'Brian Consultants; OH, Owen Hennigar; PR, Pete Replinger; RE, R. E. Swanson; RP, Rayonier Photo; TA, Tony Archer; VC, Vancouver City Archives; VI, Vancouver Island Photo-Graphics; VP, Vancouver Public Library; WB, Williams Bros.; WH, W. H. Gold.

2, FS; 12, BC; 14, BC; 15, BC, BC, NY; 16, BC; 17, FS; 18, BC, BC; 19, FS; 20, BC, BC, BC; 21, BC, BC; 22, FS, FS; 23, VP; 24, VP; 26, BC, BC, BC; 27, BC, BC, VC; 28, BC, BC; 29, BC, BC; 30, BC; 31, FS, BC; 32, BC, VC; 33, BC, BC, BC, VC; 34, GB; 35, BC; 36, BC, BC; 37, BC, BC; 38, FS, FS; 39, MK; 40, BC, FS, FS; 41, FS; 42, RE, BC; 44, EG, FS; 45, RE; 46, BC; 49, BC, RE, BC, RE; 50, VC, GG; 51, BC, BC, FS, FS; 52, BC, BC, VC; 53, BC, VC; 54, BC, BC; 55, RE, GG; 56, BC, BC, BC; 57, BC, BC, FP, BC; 58, BC, MB; 59, VP, FP, BC; 60, BC, OH; 61, BF, NY; 62, CI; 64, CZ, BC, BC; 65, BC, BC; 66, BC, BC, CZ; 67, BC; 68, FS, BC; 69, BC, BC; 71, FS, FP, BC; 72, BC, FS; 73, BC; 74, VC; 75, DT; 76, BC; 78, MB; 79, FP, BC; 80, BC, DU; 81, DU; 82, BC; 83, BC, BC; 84, BF, BC; 85, BC, BC; 86, FP; 87, RP; 88, BC, FP; 89, BF, FP; 90, BC; 91, BC, NY; 92, FS, BC; 93, BF; 94, BC; 95, BC; 96, RE, BC; 97, BC, RE; 98, BC, BC, BC; 99, BC, RP; 106, RE; 107, EG; 108, RE, RE, RE, RE; 109, BC; 110, BC, BC, BC, FP; 111, BJ; 112, FP, JC; 113, PR; 114, CZ; 115, VP; 116, CI, WH, BC;117, EG; 118, FS, BC; 119, BC, BC; 120, RP, WH, CZ; 121, JC; 122, BC, BC, BC; 123, JC; 124, JC, BC; 125, BC; 126, OH; 127, JC; 128, FW, OH, JC; 129, NY; 130, FS; 131, FS; 132, JL, NY, NY, BJ, BC, NY; 133, MB, NY; 134, BC; 135, BC; 136, FP, BC; 137, BC, BC; 138, BC, BC, BC, BC, BC, BC; 139, BC, BC; 140, BC, CZ; 141, BC, JC; 142, JC; 143, RP, NY; 144, RP, FP, AR, NY, BF; 145, NY; 146, NY; 147, CZ; 148, CZ, NY; 149, CZ, CZ; 150, DT, BC; 151, BC, CS, BC; 152, MB, MB, CI; 153, NY; 154, CF; 156, TA, BC; 157, MB, BC; 158, JC, BC; 159, CP, MB; 160, MB, MB; 161, VI, VI, DT; 162, DT, JG; 163, BC, JG; 164, FS; 165, JG, OB; 166, VP; 167, BF; 168, BF, BF, BC, BF; 169, BC, BF, BC; 170, EG, EG; 171, VP, CZ, BC; 172, CZ, CZ, CZ, WB; 173, AR, NY, NY; 174, JL, JL, WB, LU, NY; 175, NY, VP; 176, FS; 177, GG; 178, RE, BC, BC; 179, BC; 180, EG, FP; 181, BC; 182, BF; 183, BC, BC; 184, MM; 185, BC; 186, MM, BC; 187, MB, LF; 188, MB, MB, BC; 189, VP, BC; 190, LF, FS, FS, DT; 191, EG, CZ; 192, VP, CI, DR, BC, BK; 193, NY; 194, BC, GN, BC; 195, BC, BC, BC, BC, GN; 196, FS; 197, FS; 198, NF, FS, BC; 199, FS, FS, FS, FS; 200, MB, FS, MB; 201, MB, MB, NY, NY, NY, NY; 202, MB, MB, DL, NY; 203, CZ, BF, BF; 204, FS, BF, FS, FS, BF; 205, EG, FS; 206, BC, BF; 207, CZ; 208, BC; 209, BC, BC, NY; 211, LU, NY; 212, FS, BC, BC, BC; 213, LU; 214, NY, CS, NY, NY, CS; 215, BC, NY, BC, BC.

Bibliography

Arctic In Color, Autumn, 1973 (article on J. Gordon Gibson).

The Birth of the Lumber Industry in British Columbia, L.B. Dixon, Provincial Archives, Victoria.

British Columbia Forest Policy, 1909-1910, B.C. Forest Service library, Victoria, B.C.

British Columbia Recalled, Pethick and Im Baumgarten, Hancock House, Saanichton, B.C.

British Columbia Royal Commission on Forest Resources, 1957.

Canadian Imperial Bank of Commerce Newsletter, May, 1971.

Chronology of British Columbia Forest Industries, 1778 to 1969, *B.C. Lumberman Magazine* (source) published by Journal of Commerce, 1970, Vancouver, B.C.

Crown Charges for Early Timber Rights (First Report of the Task Force on Crown Timber Disposal, February, 1974). Minister of Lands, Forests & Water Resources, Victoria, B.C.

Early Lumbering on Vancouver Island, 1844-1886, by W. Kaye Lamb, Provincial Archives, Victoria, B.C.

Forest History & Policy in British Columbia (talk given by L.F. Swannell, August 14, 1967 to forestry graduates).

Frontier Days of Vancouver Island, Norcross & Tonkin.

Glory Days of Logging, Andrews, Superior Publishing, Seattle, Wash.

Government & the Forest Industry, Ted Stevens, B.C. Logging News, May, 1974.

Greenbook, various editions, Journal of Commerce, Vancouver.

A Guide of Forest Tenures in B.C., Stevens & Gormely, B.C. Logging News, February, 1974.

A History of Coquitlam and Fraser Mills, Monk & Stewart.

History of Log Towing in B.C. (unpublished UBC thesis) by C.R. Matheson, Vancouver.

History of Railroad Logging, Robert E. Swanson, Queen's Printer, Victoria, B.C.

The International Woodworkers of America in British Columbia, (IWA history), IWA head office, Vancouver, B.C.

Latest Developments in Falling and Bucking Logs, 1936, by J.A. Addison, Port Alberni, B.C.

Logger's Handbook 1973, Pacific Logging Congress, Portland, Oregon.

The Logging Labor Force in Coastal British Columbia, Research Branch, B.C. Department of Labor, Legislative Buildings, Victoria, B.C.

MacMillan Bloedel News, February, 1974 (Moving logs in northern waters).

Markets & Capital: A History of the Lumber Industry in British Columbia by J.C. Lawrence, unpublished UBC thesis, 1951.

New Zealand Official Yearbook, 1969 (Captain Cook's Voyages in the Pacific), Vancouver Public Library.

Newspapers, various issues: *Vancouver Sun, New Westminster Columbian, Vancouver Province, Cowichan Leader, Victoria Times, Victoria Daily Colonist*.

Northwest Territories Information, Yellowkife, NWT.

Ocean Highway, company promotional booklet, Island Tug & Barge, Victoria, B.C. (now Seaspan International Ltd.).

Pioneer Days of Port Renfrew, Josephine Godman.

Power Versus Handfalling and Bucking (Crown Zellerbach News, Portland, Oregon).

Raincoast Chronicles, periodical, B.C. Coast Historical Society, Madeira Park, B.C.

Samwell's Journal of Cook's Voyages, 1778. Vancouver Public Library.

Sloan Report, 1945, King's Printer, 1945.

Sloan Report, 1956, Queen's Printer, Victoria, 1957.

Sound Heritage, Volume III, Number 2, 1974, Provincial Archives, Victoria, B.C.

The Timberman Magazine, Number 12, Volume 34, October, 1933, Timberman, Portland, Oregon.

Tough Timber (unionizing logging) by Myrtle Bergren, Duncan, B.C.

Truck Logger Convention Issue, January, 1960, Gordon Black Publications, Vancouver; also, *Truck Logger Annual*, December, 1965.

Vancouver Island Railroads, Robert D. Turner, Golden West Books.

Vancouver Recalled, by Derek Pethick, Hancock House, Saanichton, B.C.

Woodsmen of the West, M. Allerdale Grainger, New Canadian Library.

Index